Many Gifts

Social Studies for Catholic Schools

Blessed Trinity York CDSB

Sylvia Pegis Santin

Patrick Gallagher

gagelearning

© 2002 Gage Learning Corporation

1120 Birchmount Road

Toronto ON M1K 5G4

1-800-668-0671

www.nelson.com

National Library of Canada Cataloguing in Publication Data

Santin, Sylvia Pegis, 1939-

    Many Gifts-Social Studies for Ontario Catholic Schools

    ISBN 0-7715-8004-5

1. Social sciences — Juvenile literature. I. Title.

H95.S38 2001   300   C2001-930003-4

Many Gifts Advisory Team

Most Reverend Marcel Gervais, Archbishop of Ottawa

Andrea Bishop, Halton Catholic District School Board

Angelo Bolotta, Toronto Catholic District School Board

Marilynn Childerhose, Dufferin-Peel Catholic District School Board

Brian DePiero, Thunder Bay Catholic District School Board

John Podgorski, Ottawa-Carleton Catholic District School Board

Reverend Michael Ryan, Former Vice Rector, St. Peter's Seminary Professor, Moral Theology

Anne O'Brien, Grey Sisters of the Immaculate Conception

Larry Trafford, Toronto Catholic District School Board

Nihil Obstat: Reverend Michael Ryan, *Censor Deputatus*, Toronto

Imprimatur: Aloysius Cardinal Ambrozic, *Archiepiscopus Torontinus*, Toronto

The Nihil Obstat and Imprimatur are official declarations that a book or pamphlet is free of doctrinal or moral error. No implication is contained therein that those who have granted the Nihil Obstat and Imprimatur agree with the contents, opinions or statements expressed.

Acknowledgements

Every reasonable effort has been made to trace ownership of copyrighted material. Information that would enable the publisher to correct any reference or credit in future editions would be appreciated.

Creative Art: Pages 175,177,178: Renné Benoit; pages 1,3,22,40,51,52,74: Heather Collins; pages 56,57,75,156,163,170: Deborah & Allan Drew-Brook-Cormack; pages 4,5,18,179,193,195: Jenny Duda; pages 60,61,204: Karen Harrison; page 43: Tina Holdcroft; pages 110, 114: June Lawrason; pages 42, 86, 104, 144: Jock MacRae; pages 101, 131, 132, 140: Jock McMaster; page 45:Ken Suzana; page 141: Sasha Warunkiw; pages 12, 17, 19, 23, 26, 30, 33, 37, 39, 41, 48, 49, 53, 80, 84, 86, 96-97, 99, 105, 109, 112, 113, 116, 124, 125, 127, 129, 130, 133, 138, 145, 147, 148, 150, 151, 152, 154, 155, 157, 165, 171, 174, 175, 181, 185, 187: ArtPlus.

Photographs: p. 6 top left © Phil Norton/VALAN PHOTOS; p. 6 bottom left © Winston Fraser; p. 6 right Charles Orrico/SuperStock; p. 7 top left © Jean Bruneau/VALAN PHOTOS; p. 7 top right © Jean Bruneau/VALAN PHOTOS; p. 7 bottom left Tom Rosenthal/SuperStock; p. 7 bottom right © Bill Wittman; p. 8 National Archives of Canada/C-6513; p. 9 National Archives of Canada/C-8007; p. 13 Canadian Press/Frank Gunn; p. 15 left and right Courtesy of PEN Canada; p. 24 Duncan R. Campbell/National Archives of Canada/PA-129249; p. 25 top right Canadian Press/Ken Gigliotti; p. 25 bottom left Canadian Press/Joe Gibbons; p. 25 bottom right Courtesy of Canadian War Museum; p. 26 © Carl Bigras/VALAN PHOTOS; p. 28 Canadian Press/Tom Hanson; p. 31 Courtesy of the Department of Canadian Heritage. Reproduced with the permission of the Minister of Public Works and Government Services Canada, 2001; p. 32 Courtesy of Senator Peggy Butts; p. 34 Photo courtesy of Phillippe Landreville Inc. © Supreme Court of Canada; p. 36 Courtesy of the Famous 5 Foundation. Sculpture by Barbara Paterson. Photograph by Jean Becq; p. 41 Canadian Press/Peter Power; p. 42 © Dick Hemingway; p. 44 Canadian Press/Kevin Frayer; p. 46 © Bill Wittman; p. 47 © Carl Bigras/VALAN PHOTOS; p. 48 © Winston Fraser; p. 50 Duncan R. Campbell/National Archives of Canada/ C-36222; p. 52 Courtesy of Romero House; p. 54 Canadian Press/Ron Poling; p. 55 © The Estate of John McNeill; p. 58 © J. Eastcott/Y. Momatiuk/VALAN PHOTOS; p. 59 top left © Dick Hemingway; p. 59 top right © Bill Wittman; p. 59 bottom left Canadian Press/Ryan Remiorz; p. 63 © Tod Gipstein/CORBIS/Magma Photo; p. 64 © Bill Wittman; p. 66 Solomon D. Butcher Collection, Nebraska State Historical Society, Neg. #B983-1653; p. 67 top left Glenbow Museum, Calgary/NA-3041-2; p. 67 top right Provincial Archives of British Columbia/HP-72553; p. 67 bottom right Glenbow Museum, Calgary/NA-5589-1; p. 68 top left National Archives of Canada/C-015568; p. 68 top right National Archives of Canada/C-6908; p. 68 bottom left © The Estate of John McNeill; p. 68 bottom right Canadian Press/Fred Chartrand; p. 69 Canadian Press/Andre Forget; p. 70 © Dick Hemingway; p. 71 top © Val & Al Wilkinson/VALAN PHOTOS; p. 71 bottom © Phil Norton/VALAN PHOTOS; p. 72 Courtesy of Joan Simone; p. 73 © Jacques M. Chenet/CORBIS/Magma Photo; p. 79 © J. Eastcott/Y. Momatiuk/VALAN PHOTOS; p. 80 Robert Aberman/Barbara Heller/Art Resource, NY; p. 81 Eberhard Streichan/SuperStock; p. 82-83 David Forbert/SuperStock; p.83 top four images Nigel Hicks/SuperStock; p. 84 Private Collection/Bridgeman Art Library; p. 85 top left & top right © J.A. Wilkinson/VALAN PHOTOS; p. 85 bottom © Gianni Dagli Orti/CORBIS/Magma Photo; p. 87 Athens Museum, Athens/Silvio Fiore/SuperStock; p. 88 © Jonathan Blair/CORBIS/Magma Photo; p. 89 Courtesy of Krzysztof Grzymski; p. 92 © Barb & Ron Kroll; p. 93 Erich Lessing/Art Resource, NY; p. 94 left British Museum, London/Bridgeman Art Library, London/SuperStock; p. 94 right Staatliche Museum, Berlin, Germany/The Bridgeman Art Library; p. 95 top left © Karen Taylor; p. 95 right Rijksmuseum Vincent Van Gogh, Amsterdam, Netherlands/Three Lions Collection/SuperStock; p. 95 bottom left Cairo, Egypt/Three Lions Collection/SuperStock; p. 98 Ancient Art and Architecture Collection Ltd./Bridgeman Art Library; p. 102 Sylvia Ford/SuperStock; p. 106 © Michel Bourque/VALAN PHOTOS; p. 107 Steve Vidler/SuperStock; p. 109 top Museum of Baghdad, Baghdad, Iraq/Silvio Fiore/SuperStock; p. 109 middle Hermitage Museum, St. Petersburg, Russia/Leonid Bogdanov/SuperStock; p. 111 National Museum of Damascus/SuperStock; p. 115 © AFP/CORBIS/Magma Photo; p. 116 Fitzwilliam Museum, Univesity of Cambridge, UK/Bridgeman Art Library; p. 117 Private Collection/Bridgeman Art Library; p. 118 Courtesy of Krzysztof Grzymski; p. 120 Courtesy of Krzysztof Grzymski; p. 121 Courtesy of Krzysztof Grzymski; p. 122 © Roger Wood/CORBIS/Magma Photo; p. 123 Erich Lessing/Art Resource, NY; p. 124 © Jonathan Blair/CORBIS/Magma Photo; p. 125 Louvre, Paris, France/Peter Willi/Bridgeman Art Library; p. 127 © Paul Almasy/CORBIS/Magma Photo; p. 128 Ashmolean Museum, Oxford, UK/Bridgeman Art Library; p. 133 © Ann Purcell/CORBIS/Magma Photo; p. 134 © Y.R. Tymstra/VALAN PHOTOS; p. 135 Steve Vidler/SuperStock; p. 136 © CORBIS/Magma Photo; p. 137 Newberry Library, Chicago/SuperStock; p. 139 © Christine Osborne/CORBIS/Magma Photo; p. 142 © Enzo & Paolor Ragazzini/CORBIS/Magma Photo; p. 146 © Charles & Josette Lenars/CORBIS/Magma Photo; p. 152 © Asian Art & Archaeology, Inc./CORBIS/Magma Photo; p. 153 Nigel Hicks/SuperStock; p. 158 Chinese, Han Dynasty, 1st to 2nd century A.D. Two Archers Mounted on Horses (from a site in Sichuan Province). Rubbing: Ink on paper. H & W: 15 1/2 x 26 3/4 in. (394 x 679 mm) AHAM 1955.41.82 © Allen Memorial Art Museum, Oberlin College, Ohio. R.T. Miller, Jr. Fund, 1955; p. 159 Michelle Burgess/SuperStock; p. 160 British Museum London/Bridgeman Art Library; p. 162 © Asian Art & Archaeology, Inc./CORBIS/Magma Photo; p. 164 Xiao Gang Shan, China Tourism Press/Getty Images; p. 166 Hulton Picture Library/Getty Images; p. 168 Musee du Louvre, Paris/ET Archive, London/SuperStock; p. 169 SuperStock; p. 171 © Ron & Barb Kroll; p. 172 © Royal Ontario Museum/CORBIS/Magma Photo; p. 173 top Peoples Republic of China/Lavros-Giraudon, Paris/SuperStock; p. 173 bottom Oriental Bronzes, Ltd., London, UK/Bridgeman Art Library; p. 182 Museo e Gallerie Nazionali di Capodimonte, Naples, Italy/Bridgeman Art Library; p. 183 Louvre, Paris, France/Index/Bridgeman Art Library; p.184 © Ron & Barb Kroll; p. 186 © Richard Nowitz/VALAN PHOTOS; p. 188 © Ron & Barb Kroll; p. 189 Scala/Art Resource, NY; p. 190 Louvre, Paris, France/Bridgeman Art Library; p. 191 Scala/Art Resource, NY; p. 192 Photofest; p. 194 Museo Archeologico Nazionale, Naples, Italy/Roger Viollet, Paris/Bridgeman Art Library; p. 196 Werner Forman Archive/Art Resource, NY; p. 197 © Kelly-Mooney Photography/CORBIS/Magma Photo; p. 198 Scala/Art Resource, NY; p. 199 Church of San Vitale, Ravenna, Italy/Canali Photo Bank, Milan/SuperStock; p. 201 © Archivo Iconographico, S.A./CORBIS/Magma Photo; p. 202 Canadian Press/AP/ Grigoris Valtinas.

We acknowledge the financial support of the Government of Canada through the Book Publishing Industry Development Program for our publishing activities.

We acknowledge the Government of Ontario through the Ontario Media Development Corporation's Ontario Book Initiative.

Creative Art Director: Donna Guilfoyle/ArtPlus Ltd.

Text Design: Leanne O'Brien/ArtPlus Ltd.

Page Layout: Sandra Sled/ArtPlus Ltd.

Cover Design: Dave Murphy/ArtPlus Ltd.

Cover Images: Heather Collins, Deborah & Allan Drew-Brook-Cormack, Jenny Duda, Jock MacRae.

ISBN 0-7715-**8004**-5

 3 4 5 TCP 06 05 04

Written, Printed, and Bound in Canada

Table of Contents

Part I

Canada's System of Government

Election Day

"Looks like a great day for an election" were the first words Ernesto Salazar heard when his clock radio came on. Canadians across the country would be voting for a new government, and now that he was 18, he would be one of them.

"Where is everyone?" he asked his mother as he walked into the kitchen. "And why is it so quiet?"

"You're up early," she said, "which is why it's so quiet. Would you go and make sure Angelina and the twins are awake?"

Before long, the kitchen was filled with people and noise. Mr. and Mrs. Salazar were talking about an order for their craft store. Angie was studying for a science test, and the twins, Rosa and Carlos, were having one of their regular arguments about whose turn it was to make their school lunches.

"*No quiero* — enough!" their mother said. "Check the schedule, and stop arguing!"

"But we like to argue," Carlos said.

"We know," their father said, "but the rest of us like peace and quiet. Besides, no arguing on election day!"

"Papi, you just made that up!" Rosa said.

"No, it's true," Angie said with a serious face. "And no arguing on a science test day either."

It took Carlos and Rosa a minute to decide she was teasing, and then they turned their attention to Ernie.

"Who are you going to choose for Prime Minister?" Rosa asked.

"Can we go with you when you vote?" Carlos asked. "I know you vote at our church because it says so on the card you got."

"I'll think about whether you can come with me," Ernie said. "And no, I'm not going to tell you whom I'm voting for. But I don't get to vote for Prime Minister."

"Why not? I thought you were old enough to vote."

"I am, but this is Canada. In the United States people vote for the person they want to be the President. We vote for Members of Parliament, and the leader of the party that wins becomes the Prime Minister."

"What's a Member of Parliament? And what does a party have to do with it?"

"Why is it different in the United States?"

"I have a question," their father said. "When are your lunches going to get made?"

"But I still don't know who Ernie's going to vote for!" Carlos said.

"I don't think you're going to find out," their mother said.

"Make your lunches," Ernie said. "Then I'll walk you to school, and you can try to get it out of me."

By the time the twins got to school, they had learned a little bit about elections. Ernie explained that:

- The Prime Minister of Canada had announced an election about six weeks earlier. The government had been in power for four years, and most people were expecting an election.

- Canada is divided into 301 *ridings*, which are areas of the country that elect one person to represent them. The 301 people elected are called *Members of Parliament*, or *MPs* for short.

- In each riding, political parties nominate people to be candidates for the election. A *political party* is a group of people who share similar ideas about how the country should be governed.

- From the day the Prime Minister announces an election until voting day, each candidate tries to convince voters that she or he is the best person to be their MP. This is called an *election campaign*.

- Before the election, cards are mailed to voters telling them the location of their *polling station*, which is the place where they vote. Buildings like churches, synagogues, schools, or community centres are often used as polling stations.

Both Rosa and Carlos thought that elections sounded interesting, but very complicated. And even though they tried to find out, they still didn't know how Ernie was going to vote.

What is Government?

Living Together

As long as people have lived in communities, they have had some form of government. To *govern* means to steer or direct. From small communities to large countries, people need to make decisions about how they will live together. Here are some examples:

"Our decision is to apply to the government for assistance to build a school. Are we all agreed?"

"The king's men better not try to collect more taxes in this village. If the king wants to go to war, he can pay for it himself."

"If elected, would your government put more money into home care for the elderly and disabled?"

"The crops have not done well this year, and soon it will be time to move. Where would be the best place for our village?"

Let's look at the example above. Without a chief, the Huron people might have had a difficult time deciding where to move their village. What if some people wanted one location, and others wanted another? The Huron people knew they needed a wise leader to steer their community, and they depended on the elders to choose this person. Once chosen, a Huron chief continued to rely on the experience and advice of older members of the community in order to make good decisions about important matters.

Life in Canada today is quite different from Huron life.

- In area, Canada is the second largest country in the world. Across this huge land, there are many ways of living. There are rural communities where fishing, farming, mining, or logging is a way of life. There are bustling cities where people live and work in a great variety of ways — manufacturing, sales, and services of all kinds. Some people commute to work on busy highways or by local trains, and others work from their homes. There are neighbourhoods within cities with a strong sense of community, and other areas where people do not know their neighbours.

- Aboriginal people have lived in Canada for thousands of years, and European settlement began hundreds of years ago. People who have been here for a very long time share a history and culture that is part of their identity. More recent immigrants are just discovering what it means to be a Canadian and how their own history and traditions fit in.

- Some Canadians are well-off, while others struggle to feed and shelter their families. Even though Canada is a wealthy country, some of its people are all too familiar with poverty, unemployment, and homelessness.

But despite these changes in the way we live, the people of Canada have the same basic human needs as communities of the past. We need:

- work, to meet our basic needs, and so that we can do our part in building a good home in God's world and in caring for all of God's people.

- safe communities in which to live.

- a just society that protects our rights and promotes the good of all.

- other people in our lives — family members, friends, community members, co-workers. God created us to love and be loved, and to work co-operatively with others to accomplish tasks that we cannot do alone.

We also need wise leaders to steer our country and make good decisions about how we will live together. This is the important responsibility of our government.

Canada's System of Government

LIVING TOGETHER: BECOMING A COUNTRY

In September 1864, political leaders from Prince Edward Island, Nova Scotia, New Brunswick, Québec (Canada East), and Ontario (Canada West) met together in Charlottetown to discuss an exciting idea: Confederation. These British colonies in North America would join together to form a new country!

Confederation wasn't going to be easy. After all, the colonies were used to running their own affairs. What would they be giving up by uniting? What would they be gaining?

But the world was changing and the colonies faced new challenges. Their leaders thought that, by joining together, they would be stronger and better able to help each other. But reaching a common agreement was a long process. They argued, they debated, they lost and won elections about joining together.

Finally, on July 1, 1867, booming cannons and parades announced the birth of the new Dominion of Canada. Nova Scotia, New Brunswick, Québec, and Ontario had joined together to form a country. Each year on this date we celebrate Confederation and our life together as Canadian citizens.

" ... we have become a people, able from our union, our strength, our population, and the development of our resources, to take our position among the nations of the world."

John A. Macdonald was a major figure in the discussions that led to the birth of Canada. He went on to become Canada's first Prime Minister.

"We sealed our federal pact without bloodshed and without exploitation of the weak by the strong. All it took was fairness, justice, and some compromise on both sides."

George-Étienne Cartier led the campaign for Confederation in Canada East (Québec). He was Macdonald's most trusted partner in the first federal government elected in Canada.

July 1 is also a day to remember the vision of the founders of our country — "fairness, justice, and some compromise on both sides." Without these ideals, Confederation might easily have failed, since there were many divisions to overcome. There were:

- **Regional differences** — The Atlantic colonies were very small in comparison to the heavily populated colonies of Canada West and East. Would Confederation serve their needs? Would their priorities and concerns matter to the rest of Canada?
- **Religious differences** — Both Canada West and Canada East had passed legislation creating publicly supported schools for religious minority groups. Under Confederation, would these rights for Catholics and Protestants continue to be respected?
- **Language and cultural differences** — The two founding European nations of Canada — France and Britain — were divided by language, culture, and religion. Would they be able to live together in a united Canada, each respecting the uniqueness of the other?

Confederation did not make these differences disappear. Instead, it recognized and protected these differences, so that the people of the colonies might join together without losing their identity. For example, in Ontario where Catholics were a minority, their right to publicly supported Catholic schools was included in the legislation that created Canada.

Confederation is an event that took place in 1867, but it is also a process that continues today. The unity and well-being of Canada depends on our commitment to the ideals of its founders — fairness, justice, compromise, and respect for differences.

Canada's system of government has some characteristics that are shared by many other countries. It is *democratic, representative,* and *federal.*

democratic — A democratic government is one that is elected and controlled by the people. The word *democracy* comes from two Greek words meaning "people" and "rule." In Canada, we have the right and the responsibility to choose our government. If we disagree with the way the government is steering the country, we can vote for new leaders during an election.

representative — We choose leaders to make decisions for us — what laws to pass, how to deal with issues like health care, taxes, the environment, unemployment, and so on. We do not vote on these issues ourselves, but elect representatives to meet together and make decisions on our behalf.

federal — In a federal system of government, the powers and responsibilities of steering the country are divided into different levels. Because Canada is a union (or federation) of ten provinces and three territories, there are two main levels of government:

- the *federal* or *national* government
- the governments of the provinces and territories, known as *provincial* or *territorial* governments

The provinces give some of their powers and responsibilities to smaller areas, like cities, towns, and villages. This third level of government is called:

- *local* or *municipal* government.

There are other features of our system of government that come from our history as British colonies. Canada is a *constitutional monarchy* and uses a *parliamentary system* of government.

constitutional monarchy — In a constitutional monarchy, the head of the country (also called the *head of state*) is a king or queen. The Prime Minister is the head of government. In Canada, our head of state is Queen Elizabeth, the ruler of the United Kingdom. In the past, rulers had unlimited power, but today Queen Elizabeth has only those powers given to her in our *constitution*. This is a written document that describes how the country is to be governed, the powers of government, and the rights of citizens. Since Queen Elizabeth lives in England, she is represented in Canada by the Governor General, who lives in Rideau Hall in Ottawa.

parliamentary system — *Parliament* is the body responsible for making laws in Canada, and is made up of the House of Commons, the Senate, and the Governor General of Canada. The members of the House of Commons, called Members of Parliament (MPs), are elected by the people. Senators are chosen by the Prime Minister and represent all regions of the country. Together, these people — MPs, Senators, and the Governor General — are responsible for governing Canada.

Canada's Coat of Arms

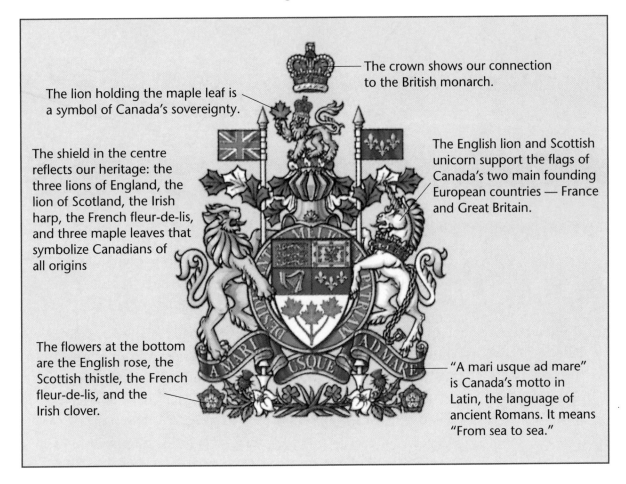

The crown shows our connection to the British monarch.

The lion holding the maple leaf is a symbol of Canada's sovereignty.

The shield in the centre reflects our heritage: the three lions of England, the lion of Scotland, the Irish harp, the French fleur-de-lis, and three maple leaves that symbolize Canadians of all origins

The English lion and Scottish unicorn support the flags of Canada's two main founding European countries — France and Great Britain.

The flowers at the bottom are the English rose, the Scottish thistle, the French fleur-de-lis, and the Irish clover.

"A mari usque ad mare" is Canada's motto in Latin, the language of ancient Romans. It means "From sea to sea."

There is another important feature of government in Canada that is shared by many other countries: *political parties*.

political parties — A *political party* is a group of people with similar ideas about how the country should be governed. These ideas are laid out in a *party platform* that explains what the group stands for and how it would act on important issues.

Canada, like most democratic countries, has a number of political parties. This means that voters have a choice among different ideas about how the country should be governed. In Ernie Salazar's riding, there are six candidates who want to be the next MP. Each belongs to a political party and is running on the platform of that party.

MAJOR POLITICAL PARTIES IN CANADA

These are the symbols of the five main political parties in Canada at the time of the federal election in 2000. The leaders of political parties are chosen from among their members. The party that elects the most MPs usually forms the government, and its leader becomes the Prime Minister. There are also a number of smaller political parties in Canada who nominate candidates to run in elections.

OTHER SYSTEMS OF GOVERNMENT

There are a number of other democratic countries that are constitutional monarchies. Australia and New Zealand both recognize Queen Elizabeth as their monarch. Like Canada, these countries were once British colonies.

Canada, Australia, and New Zealand belong to an association of countries called the Commonwealth of Nations. This association has 54 members and meets regularly to discuss world peace, trade, international aid, and other common concerns. Every four years, one of the member countries hosts the Commonwealth Games in which athletes compete in a variety of sports.

Japan is another example of a constitutional monarchy. This country has its own royal family, with the Emperor as the head of state. Like Canada, Japan elects representatives, the party with the most votes forms the government, and its leader becomes the Prime Minister.

The governments of the United States of America and of Canada have several features in common. Both are democracies, with elected representatives chosen by the people, and both have a federal system of government. The United States is a union of 50 states, with two levels of government — federal (national) and state. Like Canada, the states share their powers with smaller areas, like towns and cities. Unlike Canada, however, the United States is a republic, not a constitutional monarchy. Its citizens vote directly for their President, who is both the head of state and the head of government.

Although the American colonies were once ruled by Britain, they rebelled and fought for their independence. One of the first tasks of the newly independent country was to write a constitution that explained how the country was to be governed. Here are some examples of differences between the systems of government in Canada and the United States:

- Instead of a Parliament, the body that makes laws in the United States is called *Congress*. It is made up of an elected Senate, with two senators from each state, and an elected House of Representatives, with 435 members. The number of representatives varies from 1 for states with small populations to 52 for California, which has the largest number of citizens.

- The President and his main advisers (his Cabinet) are not members of Congress. Since the people who wrote the Constitution of the United States did not want to give too much power to any individual or group, the powers of the President are separate from the powers of Congress. For example, the President can *veto*, or reject, legislation passed by Congress. But if two-thirds of the Senate and the House of Representatives vote in favour of the legislation, it becomes law despite the President's veto.

- The two main political parties in the United States are the Democrats and the Republicans. Because the President is elected directly, he may belong to one political party while Congress has a majority of members from the other party. When this happens, it is often difficult for the President to convince Congress to pass legislation.

- American presidents are elected for a four-year term and cannot be defeated during that time. So even without the support of the majority of Congress, the President remains in office for the entire term. American presidents, however, can only serve for two terms.

In countries like Canada and the United States, which have always been democratic, citizens often take their freedom for granted. There are many places in the world where the right to speak freely, to practise one's religion, to elect the government, or to be treated fairly in a court of law does not exist.

A country where one person or group controls all of the power is usually called a *dictatorship*. A *dictator* is a person who has absolute authority. In a dictatorship:

- There is no constitution that limits the powers of government and protects the rights of citizens.

- There are no free elections. Some dictatorships call themselves democratic and hold elections, but citizens do not have a real choice in electing representatives.

- There are no independent courts where a citizen can have a fair trial.

- Media, such as newspapers, radio, and television, are controlled by those in power. Public criticism of the government is not allowed.

Organizations like Amnesty International and PEN Canada gather information and inform people about abuses of human freedom that occur around the world. PEN members work to free those who have been imprisoned for what they have written or said. Here are some people that PEN Canada has been involved with:

Tesfaye Deressa is a poet, writer, and songwriter in Ethiopia, charged with treason and violating the Ethiopian Press Laws.

Daw San San Nweh is a writer in Myanmar, imprisoned for 10 years for "spreading information injurious to the state."

People who have lived in a dictatorship, and later moved to a democratic country, know what it is like to live without basic human rights. They cherish the freedom of their new land and never take it for granted.

Choosing a Government

When Ernie heard that there was to be an election, he was quite excited. He was interested in politics, and now that he was 18 years old, he could finally vote.

The Election Process

Calling an election — In Canada, federal elections must be held at least once every five years. But the Prime Minister may decide not to wait that long. It could be as short a time as three years, but often it is about four years. Here are two reasons a Prime Minister might decide to call an election early:

- There are important issues facing the country, and people need an opportunity to discuss and vote on them.

- Everything is going well in the country, and the Prime Minister's political party has a good chance of winning and forming the government again.

Although the Prime Minister makes the decision, calling an election requires the consent of the Queen's representative in Canada, the Governor General. If the Governor General agrees, which almost always happens, Parliament is dissolved, and the House of Commons and the Senate no longer meet. A new Parliament begins after the next election.

Becoming a candidate — Exactly four weeks before the election, a list is made of all candidates. Let's imagine that a woman named Louise Brown who lives in the riding of West River wants to be a candidate. She meets the basic requirements:

- She is at least 18 years old.

- She is a Canadian citizen.

- She lives in Canada.

How does she get her name on the list?

Canada is divided into 301 ridings, which are also called *electoral districts* or *constituencies*. These ridings correspond to the 301 *seats* in the House of Commons. Each riding elects one MP to the House of Commons.

Almost all candidates in a federal election belong to a political party and are nominated by that party. In order to be a candidate, Louise must be nominated in her riding. Also, at least 100 voters from this riding must sign her nomination papers. Since she has been active in her community and her political party, she is successful. Louise is now the candidate for her party in the imaginary riding of West River.

Political Ridings in Canada

As you can see, the provinces of Ontario and Québec, with the largest populations, have the most seats in the House of Commons. Some parts of Canada have a small number of people spread out across a large area, and other parts have thousands of people living in just one neighbourhood of a big city. Riding boundaries have to take these differences into account. If each riding were exactly the same size, one MP might represent a thousand people, and another might represent more than a million. Would this be fair?

Campaigning — Each candidate prepares a *campaign*, which is a series of activities designed to help him or her get elected. Voters need to know who the person is, what qualifications he or she has to be an MP, and what ideas the person has about governing the country. Here are just some of the campaign activities of candidates.

- They participate in public meetings where all candidates in a riding present their party's platform on the issues and answer voters' questions.

- They visit homes, schools, shopping malls, and other places to talk to voters.

- They distribute brochures that inform voters about who they are, why they are running, and what they stand for.

- They put up signs with their name and political party.

- They telephone voters and ask for their support.

The national leaders of the main political parties are even busier. As well as campaigning in their own ridings, they also travel to every region of the country to try to convince voters to elect candidates from their political party. They debate each other on television, appear on radio shows, and are the subject of many newspaper articles. In this way, Canadians get a good look at the people who want to be the next Prime Minister of Canada.

Voting — When the campaign is over, it is time for the people of Canada to choose their MPs. A week or so before election day, voters receive cards in the mail telling them the location of their *polling station*, the place where they vote. To be eligible to vote, people must be at least 18 years old and Canadian citizens.

Here is what happens at the polling station:

- The voter gives the card to the *polling clerk*, who crosses the person's name off the voter list. Each name is crossed off so that no one can vote more than once.

- The person in charge of the polling station, called the *deputy returning officer*, gives the voter a *ballot*, which is a piece of paper with the names of the candidates in the riding and their political parties.

- The voter takes the ballot to a small table with a cardboard screen on it, and marks an X beside the name of the person he or she wants to elect. The screen is used to prevent anyone from seeing how people vote. Elections in Canada are by secret ballot.

- The voter then puts the ballot in a ballot box along with all the others from that polling station.

Mario Conforti ◯
(Party A)

Louise Brown ◯
(Party B)

Richard O'Brien ◯
(Party C)

Angela DaSouza ⊗
(Party D)

Tara Singh Malik ◯
(Party E)

After the polling station closes, the ballot box is opened under supervised conditions, and the votes are counted. Great care is taken to make sure the final numbers are accurate. The results from each polling station are reported to the *returning officer*, who is the person in charge of the election for a whole riding.

The Election Results

As the votes are counted and polling stations report their results to the returning officers of the ridings, the candidates wait and wonder: "Will I be successful? Did I manage to convince the voters that I would be the best person? Did I do a good job of explaining why my party's platform is what Canada needs?"

Winning or losing — Our imaginary candidate, Louise Brown, is waiting. When the first results from a few polling stations are reported, she is very pleased.

West River Riding (5 out of 157 polls reporting)		
Party A	Mario Conforti	317
Party B	Louise Brown	402
Party C	Richard O'Brien	89
Party D	Angela DaSouza	101
Party E	Tara Singh Malik	113

But as results from other polling stations come in, Louise is disappointed. Mario Conforti is gaining votes. By the time all the results are in, Mario is the winner. He will be the next MP for West River.

West River Riding (157 out of 157 polls reporting)		
Party A	Mario Conforti	12 910
Party B	Louise Brown	10 233
Party C	Richard O'Brien	2 422
Party D	Angela DaSouza	4 155
Party E	Tara Singh Malik	3 382

Forming a government — The political party that elects the most candidates across the country almost always forms the government. In our imaginary election, we already know that Mario Conforti has been elected in the riding of West River. But what about the other 300 ridings?

Final Election Results (301 ridings): Majority Government				
Party A	**Party B**	**Party C**	**Party D**	**Party E**
57	163	16	24	41

Party B has won the election, and will form the next government, with its leader as the Prime Minister. It will be a *majority government*, which means Party B has won more than half of the 301 seats in the House of Commons. With this majority, the government will be able to propose and pass legislation with little difficulty. Even if all the MPs from the other four parties were to vote against the government's legislation, they would not have enough votes to defeat it.

But what if the results of the election had looked like this?

Final Election Results (301 ridings): Minority Government				
Party A	**Party B**	**Party C**	**Party D**	**Party E**
71	137	16	36	41

Party B is still the winner of the election, but it has less than half of the 301 seats in the House of Commons. The new government will be a *minority government*. Since it has only 137 seats in the House of Commons, it will need to convince some members of the other parties to vote with the government in order to pass legislation. If it cannot convince them, the government will be defeated and must resign. The other parties may try to form a government by winning support from each other. If none of them can form a government, there will be another election.

Levels of Government

The Federal Government

"If I can guess the person you're going to vote for, will you tell me if I'm right?" Rosa asked Ernie.

"Nope."

"Does that mean you're never going to tell us?" Carlos asked. "That's not fair."

"You two!" their mother said. "You never stop!"

"Carlos, Rosa! Come help with dinner," their father called.

It was late afternoon, and Mr. and Mrs. Salazar and Angie had just arrived home from the store. Ernie and Angie took turns helping in the store after school.

"How was the science test?" Ernie asked Angie.

"Pretty hard," she said. "But I think I did all right. So, have you decided whom you're going to vote for?"

"Not you, too!"

"Just kidding. But, seriously, I think you should vote for someone who's going to do something about pollution. What's more important than clean air and water?"

"I know it's important, but so are jobs, people without homes, fair taxes, helping poorer countries," Ernie said. "There's a lot to think about."

"Well, my vote would go to clean air and water," Angie replied.

We elect a federal government to make wise decisions about how we will live together as Canadians.

- Will we have clean air and water?
- Will people have work and places to live?
- What taxes are needed to meet our common needs?

These are only some of the issues that the federal government must face as it steers our country into the future.

The federal government has three main responsibilities that are met by three branches of government:

- *legislative branch* — makes laws
- *executive branch* — develops policies and legislation, looks after the day-to-day business of governing the country, and provides services to Canadians
- *judicial branch* — applies and interprets laws

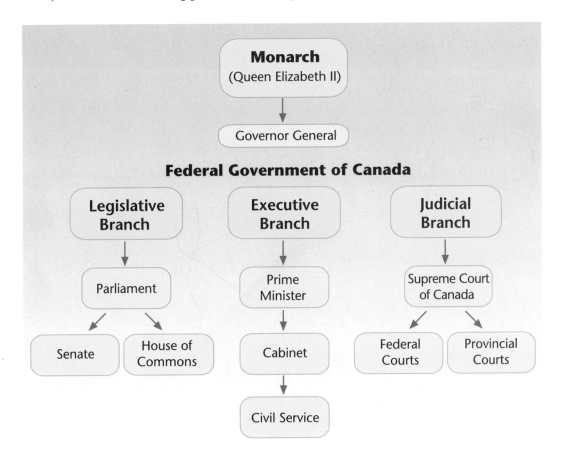

Executive Branch

The executive branch develops policies, introduces legislation, and supervises those who carry out government plans. The Prime Minister, the Cabinet, and members of the civil service make up the executive branch of the federal government.

Prime Minister — The Prime Minister is an elected MP, represents a riding, and is the leader of the political party in power. The Prime Minister is also the head of government, and represents the country abroad. It is the Prime Minister's responsibility to develop policies and legislation that best serve the people of Canada. This enormous task requires a group of capable advisers, called the *Cabinet*.

Cabinet — The Cabinet is a group of MPs chosen by the Prime Minister to give advice and to share the responsibilities of leadership. Cabinet members are called *ministers*, and are usually given special responsibility for one area of government — Minister of the Environment, Minister of Health, Minister of Justice, and so on.

In 1957, under Prime Minister John Diefenbaker, Ellen Fairclough became the first woman Cabinet minister in Canada.

The Prime Minister and the Cabinet meet regularly. During these meetings, which are private, Cabinet members may sometimes disagree with each other or with the Prime Minister. The Cabinet looks at all sides of an issue, and carefully considers proposed legislation. Once a decision has been reached, however, all Cabinet members must support it publicly. If a minister cannot support the policies of the government, he or she must resign from the Cabinet.

The Prime Minister and the Cabinet are responsible to the House of Commons. If the other members of the House do not have confidence in the way these leaders are steering the country, they have the power to defeat the government. This is called a vote of non-confidence.

Civil Service — Suppose you are an immigrant to Canada, and want to find out how to become a citizen. Or you are researching work in Canada, and want to find out how many people are looking for employment. Or perhaps you plan to travel to another country and need a passport. The people who can help you are employed by the government of Canada, and are called *civil servants* or *public servants*.

Civil servants are responsible for the day-to-day work of the government. They serve the people of Canada — the public — by carrying out the federal government's policies and programs. Here are just a few examples of their work.

working to protect the health of Canadians, like this scientist at the Disease Control Centre in Winnipeg

delivering mail across Canada

acting as guides in Canada's heritage sites

Legislative Branch

The Parliament Buildings, which are the main home of our federal government, are located in Ottawa, the capital of Canada.

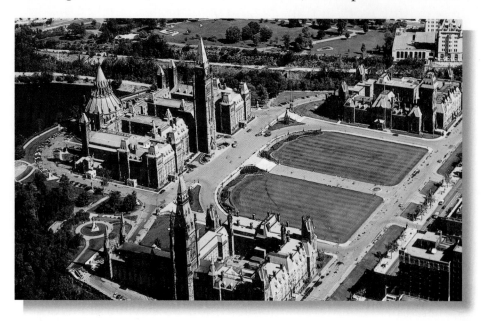

Our elected representatives meet in the House of Commons to debate and pass legislation.

The House of Commons

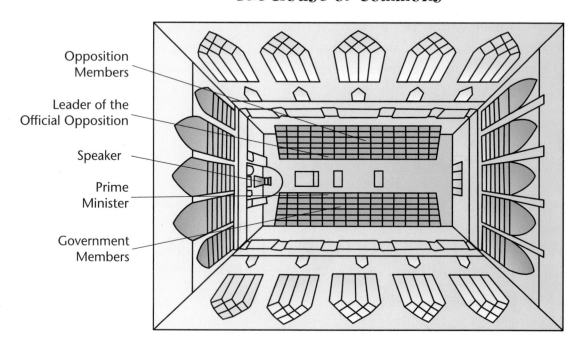

Opposition Members

Leader of the Official Opposition

Speaker

Prime Minister

Government Members

Only legislation that falls under the powers and responsibilities of the federal government can be proposed. These include:

- immigration
- agriculture and fisheries
- banking and issuing money
- international relations
- transportation
- Native people and reserved lands
- postal service
- armed forces and defence
- direct and indirect taxation
- criminal justice
- trade and commerce
- environment

Imagine 301 MPs discussing and voting on an important issue such as how to preserve fish stocks. They represent different regions and have a variety of opinions. They want an opportunity to present their views, but if they all talk at once, nothing would be accomplished. Clear rules are needed.

Look at the diagram on page 26, and imagine that you are the Speaker of the House, seated at one end of the main chamber. If you look to your right, you will see the government members, and to your left, the opposition. Seated in the galleries around the chamber are journalists, special visitors, and the public.

Government members —The political party with the largest number of MPs usually forms the government, and its members sit together on the right side of the House. The Prime Minister and members of the Cabinet sit in the front row.

Opposition members — The political party with the second largest number of MPs forms the *Official Opposition*, and its members sit on the left side of the House. The leader and his or her most important advisers sit in the front row.

MPs from the other political parties also sit on the left side, and are part of the opposition, but not the Official Opposition. The opposition questions the policies of the government, examines proposed legislation and suggests improvements, and proposes new ideas about governing the country.

Speaker of the House — At the front of the chamber is the Speaker of the House, who is the presiding officer. The Speaker is something like a referee — he or she enforces the rules. For example, MPs cannot speak whenever they want, but must be called on by the Speaker. Making sure that all members of the House both act and are treated fairly and respectfully is an important responsibility.

The Speaker also represents the House of Commons in meetings with provincial governments and with the parliaments of other countries.

In the past, the government chose the Speaker and the members of the House voted to confirm the person; but since 1986 the Speaker has been elected by all MPs in a secret ballot. This change is a way of recognizing that it is the MPs who give and accept the special authority of their Speaker.

It is not an easy task to be the Speaker of the House. Just like a referee, the Speaker, although a member of a political party, cannot take sides, but must act fairly toward all members.

When the House of Commons is in session, the day begins with the Speaker's parade. The *Mace*, a large, decorated gold club, is carried into the House of Commons by the Sergeant-at-Arms, who is followed by the Speaker. The Mace symbolizes the authority of Parliament, and is placed on a table in front of the Speaker's chair. In the Middle Ages, a mace was carried as a weapon by the king's bodyguard.

The House is in session — When the House is in session, MPs gather for a meeting each day, starting with a prayer read by the Speaker. Then the regular business begins. This might include:

- the introduction of a new bill by the government.

- reports from committees.

- discussion and debate on a bill that was introduced earlier.

- a final vote on a bill that has already been debated.

There is also time set aside each day for members of the opposition to question the Prime Minister and the Cabinet. These questions are supposed to be brief, concern important matters, and seek information. Since MPs sometimes use Question Period as an opportunity to make speeches or to try to embarrass the government, the Speaker is kept very busy enforcing the rules.

V O T I N G   I N   T H E   H O U S E   O F   C O M M O N S

When MPs vote in the House of Commons, they are expected to vote with their party. But what if an MP strongly disagrees with the position of his or her party on an important matter? When this happens, an MP may decide to quit the party, and sit in the House as an independent member.

On a few occasions, proposed legislation may involve serious moral issues. Since a person's views on such issues involve deeply held beliefs about what is right and wrong, party leaders recognize that MPs must be given the freedom to vote according to their conscience. In 1987, a free vote was held on the issue of capital punishment, which had been abolished in Canada in 1976. By a vote of 148 to 127, MPs reaffirmed Canada's position: People convicted of serious crimes, such as murder, cannot be executed as a punishment. Canada is one of 67 countries in the world that has completely abolished capital punishment.

From bill to law — The government wants to introduce a *bill* to protect endangered species. A bill is a piece of proposed legislation. It must pass through a number of stages in order to become a law.

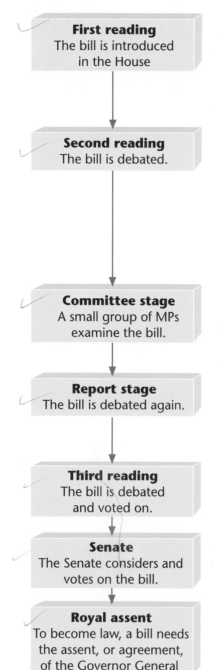

First reading
The bill is introduced in the House

Second reading
The bill is debated.

Committee stage
A small group of MPs examine the bill.

Report stage
The bill is debated again.

Third reading
The bill is debated and voted on.

Senate
The Senate considers and votes on the bill.

Royal assent
To become law, a bill needs the assent, or agreement, of the Governor General

- **First reading** — The MP responsible for the bill introduces it and asks that it be given first reading, which means that the members agree to consider it. If the bill is accepted, it is printed and distributed to the other MPs.

- **Second reading** — Several weeks later, the MP who introduced the bill gives a speech explaining its main purpose. Then debate begins, and opposition members criticize the bill. If they are strongly opposed, they try to delay its being passed. If the bill passes the vote at this stage, it is referred to a committee for careful study.

- **Committee stage** — The committee that studies the bill has MPs from all political parties. It is their job to examine it and propose changes, called *amendments*, and prepare a report for the House.

- **Report stage** — The amended bill is considered and debated. Any MP can propose further amendments, each of which must be voted on. A date is then set for a third reading.

- **Third reading** — The bill is considered and debated by the House for the last time. Then the MPs vote on the bill.

- **Senate** — Once a bill has passed, it must be sent to the Senate, where it will again be debated and voted on.

- **Royal assent** — The last stage is the assent of the Governor General. Once this is given, the bill has become law.

On December 15, 1964, Canada's flag was approved by a resolution of the House of Commons. The vote was 163 for and 78 against. Two days later, the Senate also approved the flag. Queen Elizabeth herself issued this proclamation, which declared that from February 15, 1965, the flag that you see in the centre of the proclamation would be the National Flag of Canada. Almost 100 years after Canada was born, our country had its own flag.

The Senate — If you look back at the chart on page 23, you will see that there are two assemblies involved in the legislative branch of the federal government — the House of Commons and the Senate. The Senate, which is also called the *Upper House,* and has 105 members, who are chosen by the Prime Minister and appointed by the Governor General. The members represent all parts of Canada:

- Atlantic provinces — 30 senators
- Québec — 24 senators
- Ontario — 24 senators
- Western provinces — 24 senators
- Territories — 3 senators

When Canada first became a country, the people who wrote the Constitution believed it was important for Parliament to have an Upper House. Their model was the British Parliament, which had both a House of Commons and a House of Lords.

The Senate meets in its own chamber, and like the House of Commons, elects a Speaker to preside at its meetings. Its main role is to take a second look at legislation passed by the House of Commons, and make sure it is in the best interests of all regions of the country. The Senate often makes minor amendments to or changes legislation, but only on a few occasions has it rejected a bill.

The institution of the Senate is frequently criticized by Canadians. Some of their concerns are:

- Senate members are not accountable to the people of Canada since they are appointed rather than elected.
- Prime Ministers often use Senate appointments to reward people with strong connections to their political parties.
- The distribution of Senate seats is unfair to the four western provinces.

Some people think the Senate should be abolished. Others would like an elected Senate with an equal number of members from each province.

SENATOR PEGGY BUTTS

One evening in 1997 the phone rang while Sister Peggy Butts was watching her beloved Montreal Canadiens on television. It was Prime Minister Jean Chrétien. He told her he remembered a fiery speech she had given asking for more help for the poor, and asked her if she would be willing to join the Senate as a representative of the Atlantic region. Sister Peggy thought she might be able to do more about the problem of poverty as a senator so she agreed.

There was one problem, however. According to the Constitution, senators have to own $4000 worth of property. Because she was a nun and had taken a vow of poverty, Sister Peggy owned nothing.

Eventually, the local bishop solved the problem by giving Sister Peggy a small piece of church property, which she returned when she retired from the Senate in 1999. And that is how Sister Peggy Butts became the first Catholic nun to be a senator.

Judicial Branch

Almost 800 years ago in England, when King John's barons forced him to sign the Magna Carta, a new way of understanding the rule of law came into being: No one, not even the king, is above the law. Over time, people came to see this principle as an important protection for their freedoms and rights, and they were willing to fight and die for it. Canadians share this understanding of the rule of law. Every person, from the Prime Minister to an ordinary citizen, is subject to the law.

But who decides if someone has broken the law, and who determines the consequences? What if there are disagreements about the meaning of a law? The judicial branch of government has the responsibility of applying and interpreting the laws of Canada. This branch operates through a system of courts and judges.

Supreme Court of Canada

- Canada's highest court
- cases involve constitutional issues and appeals from lower courts

Federal Court of Canada

- trial and appeal divisions
- cases involve matters like income tax or customs duties

Provincial Superior or Supreme Courts

- trial and appeal divisions
- highest courts in the provinces
- cases involve the most serious criminal and civil matters

District or County Courts

- cases involve criminal and civil matters

Provincial Courts

- cases involve minor criminal and civil matters, and family law issues

Here are a few examples of court cases.

A province believes that a law passed by the federal government intrudes into its powers and responsibilities. The province has decided to challenge the law.

Supreme Court of Canada — This case will be heard by the Supreme Court of Canada, the country's highest court. Our Constitution gives the Supreme Court the power to decide if one level of government has gone beyond the authority given to it by the Constitution. If the judges agree with the province, the law will be struck down.

The Supreme Court has nine judges, whose leader is the Chief Justice. The Right Honourable Beverley McLachlin, seated in the centre, was appointed Chief Justice on January 7, 2000. She is the first woman to hold this position.

Supreme Court judges are appointed by the federal government, which makes sure that all regions of the country are represented. The judges cannot be dismissed unless both the House of Commons and the Senate agree. To protect the independence of our courts, judges do not have to worry about losing their jobs by making decisions that are unpopular with the government. Their responsibility is to apply and interpret the law impartially.

The Supreme Court agrees to hear only those cases that are important for the whole country, and its decisions are final. There is no other court to which a government or individual can appeal.

John has been charged with the crime of murder. He has pleaded "not guilty," and his trial will begin in a few weeks.

Provincial Superior Courts — Because of the seriousness of the crime, John's case will likely be heard by the trial division of the highest level provincial court. Criminal acts are not simply offences against individuals, but are crimes against the whole society. For this reason, they are prosecuted by the state. Since one of the basic rights of Canadian citizens is a fair trial, John has the right to be represented by a competent lawyer. If he cannot afford a lawyer, one will be provided for him by the court.

When the trial is over, if John is found guilty, he may be able to appeal his conviction. But he cannot appeal just because he is unhappy with the verdict. A provincial appeal court will not agree to hear his case unless there is some indication that he may not have received a fair or proper trial. In rare cases, decisions of provincial appeal courts can be appealed to the Supreme Court of Canada.

Emily and Mike hired a contractor to repave their driveway, and gave him a down payment. They are dissatisfied with the job, and have refused to pay the final bill. The contractor has decided to sue them for the rest of the money.

Small Claims Court — Emily and Mike's problem with their contractor is not a criminal matter. It is a civil matter — a dispute between individuals. Since it does not involve a large amount of money, this case will be heard by a provincial small claims court. The judge will listen to both sides and make a decision.

The responsibility of all courts, from the highest to the lowest, is to apply and interpret the law fairly. The courts serve the law, and by doing so protect the rights and freedoms of everyone.

LIVING TOGETHER: EQUAL RIGHTS

The family of Canada is made up of millions of people. We are recent immigrants from around the world, we are Aboriginal people, and we are people who have lived here for many generations. We are female, male, young, old, ill, healthy, disabled, and able-bodied. Together, we are the people of Canada.

In order to live together, we need to be able to count on certain freedoms and rights. Our right to be treated equally is especially important. This right is guaranteed by our Constitution in the Canadian Charter of Rights and Freedoms.

But this was not always so. There was a time in our history when women were not allowed to vote. In 1918, after a long struggle, Canadian women won the right to vote.

But there was still another hurdle to be faced. Could women be appointed to the Senate? The legislation that created Canada referred to the appointment of "qualified persons" to the Senate, but a woman had never been chosen. Did "qualified persons" include women?

In 1928, five Canadian women took this question to the Supreme Court of Canada, and its answer was no. Until 1949, however, Supreme Court decisions were not final and could be appealed to a higher court in Great Britain. The women appealed and won their case. In 1930, Cairine Wilson became the first woman senator.

This sculpture of the five women who fought for the right to be treated equally is located in Calgary. The women are Emily Murphy, Henrietta Edwards, Louise McKinney, Irene Parlby, and Nellie McClung.

Provincial Government

Canada is a federation of ten provinces and three territories. Our Constitution requires that the powers and responsibilities of governing be divided into two levels — a federal level and a provincial and territorial level. A third level — local or municipal government — is not defined in the Constitution, but is a provincial responsibility.

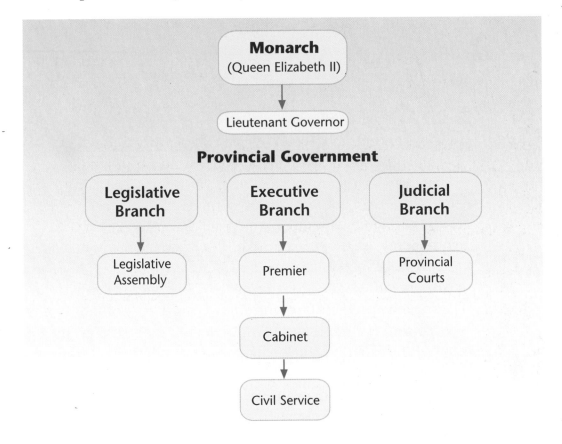

In many ways, provincial governments are similar to the federal government:

- The Queen is represented by a Lieutenant Governor.
- The Premier of a province, like the Prime Minister, is usually the leader of the party with the most elected members.
- Several titles are used for elected members, depending on the province. In Ontario they are called MPPs — Members of the Provincial Parliament.

- Provincial governments have three main responsibilities:

  1. to make laws about matters that affect the people of the province (the legislative branch)

  2. to apply and interpret the laws of the province and of Canada (judicial branch)

  3. to develop policies and legislation, and supervise the people who carry out the plans of the government (executive branch)

- Provincial elections are similar to federal elections. Candidates are nominated and the person with the most votes wins. The political party with the most elected members generally forms the government. The party with the second largest number of seats forms the Official Opposition.

- Legislation is developed by the Premier and Cabinet ministers, and is debated and voted on in the provincial legislature. The opposition questions the policies and proposed legislation of the government. If the government loses a vote on an important issue, it must resign.

If you look at the charts on pages 23 and 37, you may notice one difference between the federal government and those of the provinces. Provincial governments do not have a Senate. Once a bill has passed in the legislative assembly and received the assent of the Lieutenant Governor, it is the law of the province.

But the most important difference between the two levels of government lies in the areas for which they are responsible. The powers and responsibilities of provincial governments, which are defined in the Constitution, include:

- education
- health
- administration of the courts
- municipal institutions
- forestry, lands, and wildlife
- direct taxation

- natural resources
- provincial highways
- environment
- social services
- agriculture
- immigration

If you compare this list to the one on page 27, you will notice several areas in which both levels of government are involved. Also, the provinces have some obligations that require large amounts of money — education, health, social services. Without the help of the federal government, it would be impossible for provinces to pay for schools and hospitals, or to provide social assistance to people in need.

GOVERNING IN THE TERRITORIES

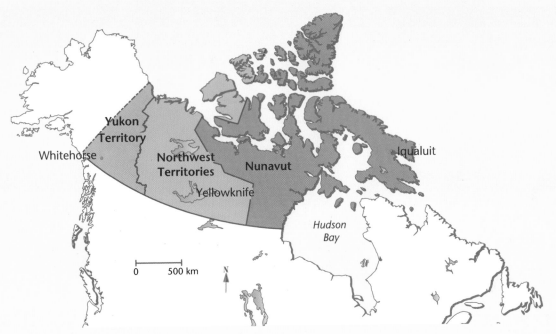

The three territories of Canada — Yukon, the Northwest Territories, and Nunavut — are governed by elected representatives. As territories, however, each has a commissioner appointed by the federal government. Over the years, the role of this person has become something like that of a Lieutenant Governor in a province. The commissioner does not generally interfere with the decisions of the elected government.

The powers and responsibilities of the territories include education, housing, social services, and renewable natural resources. Non-renewable natural resources, like minerals and fossil fuels, are under the control of the federal government.

Local Government

Here are just some of the events in the life of the Salazar family during a single week.

- Carlos and Rosa went swimming at their local recreation centre.
- The Salazars received a notice that the rent they pay for their store is going up. The reason, according to the owner, is an increase in property taxes.
- Ernie got his first parking ticket.
- Angie went to the library to get books for a school project.
- The family's dinner was interrupted by the sound of sirens. One of their neighbours had a kitchen fire. Fortunately, the firefighters were able to put it out quickly.
- Mr. and Mrs. Salazar went for a walk after dinner and noticed that the flower beds in their neighbourhood park had been cleaned up for winter.

Each of these events involves one of the services or powers of local governments. Local governments:

- offer services, like recreation centres, public libraries, parks, and fire departments.

- have the power to make and enforce laws about matters such as where and when people may park their cars.

- raise money to pay for services through property taxes.

An area that has its own elected local government is called a *municipality*. Some municipalities consist of a single urban centre, like a large city or town. Others are made up of a number of smaller rural communities.

Mayor Hazel McCallion of Mississauga celebrates winning her eighth term as mayor in November 2000.

Local Government

Mayor

Council

Municipal Staff
(public servants)

As you can see, the basic organization of local government is much simpler than that of the federal or provincial governments.

Mayor — The leader of a local government is usually called the *mayor*. Mayors are elected directly by the people, and represent their municipalities at many official functions. They also have the important responsibility of communicating with the province about the needs of their communities.

Council — Elected councillors make up the local government council. In most large urban centres, they represent a particular area of the municipality, called a *ward*. In smaller centres, the council is made up of the people who received the most votes across the whole municipality.

Municipal staff — In a large urban community, there may be thousands of people who work for the municipality, such as bus drivers, police officers, firefighters, garbage collectors, lifeguards, and librarians. In small municipalities, there are few staff members, and services like firefighting and emergency medical care are often provided by trained volunteers.
In very small or isolated communities, some services are supplied by a regional authority or by the province.

In many rural areas, the Ontario Provincial Police serve the community.

Local governments have three main responsibilities:

- to make laws, which are called *by-laws* at the local level of government. A by-law applies only in the municipality in which it was passed. Local governments pass by-laws to meet the needs of their communities.

- to enforce the laws. Local governments do not interpret the laws, since this is a federal and provincial responsibility. But they employ police officers to make sure the laws of the municipality, province, and country are obeyed.

- to provide necessary services.

Who repairs the pothole?

Who picks up your garbage?

Who looks after your local park?

Local services are so important in our daily lives that we often take them for granted. We turn on the tap and clean water comes out; flip a switch and the lights go on; go to the park for a game of soccer or to the arena to play hockey. It's only when something goes wrong — the water isn't safe to drink; there's no electric power; the parks and the arenas are closed — that we realize how important these services are.

Municipalities need money to pay for workers and services. A local government receives some financial support from its province, but must also raise a large part of its budget. Most of this money comes from property taxes paid by people who own homes and businesses. A smaller part comes from fees and licences; for example, a membership fee at a recreation centre or a dog licence. If a municipality does not have enough money, services must be cut back.

LIVING TOGETHER: ABORIGINAL PEOPLE

The way people live together and make decisions reflects their history and traditions. We were once a British colony, and when we became independent, we drew on this past to create our system of government.

The history and traditions of the Aboriginal people of Canada influence their thinking about how to live together. The custom of making decisions by consensus has a special importance to them. A *consensus* is a common agreement — one that takes into account the opinions of everyone in the group.

An example of this tradition can be seen in the approach to government in the Northwest Territories and in Nunavut. There are no political parties, and each candidate runs as an independent. Once Members of the Legislative Assembly are elected, they choose a Premier and Cabinet members from among themselves. There is no pressure to vote according to a political party position, and decisions are reached by discussion and compromise.

The Legislative Assembly building in Iqaluit. The ceiling of the chamber represents an igloo.

A question every group of people must face is what to do about lawbreakers. Aboriginal traditions emphasize the role of the community in answering this question and in helping offenders rejoin the community as trusted members.

This approach to achieving justice is used in Aboriginal communities in several areas of Canada. As well as the judge, offender, and lawyers, community members participate in discussing the consequences of the offence, and how the person might make amends and be helped to change.

Connections Among Governments

At St. Leo's School, where Carlos and Rosa are in Grade 5, there is an annual spring fair. This is a big event to organize, and takes a lot of work from everyone. Preparation is just beginning for this year's fair, and parents, students, and teachers have formed several committees. There are committees to:

- plan the schedule of activities for the day.
- invite businesses to donate items for charity raffles.
- arrange drinks and food for snacks and lunch.
- get people to help with setting up and cleaning up.

The members of each committee will need to be committed and willing to work hard to make the day a success. But hard work and good intentions, important as they are, won't be enough. The committees will also have to communicate with each other, co-ordinate their efforts, and work co-operatively to achieve their common goal — a great spring fair.

Having a great country is a lot more complicated than having a great spring fair, especially when people don't always agree on what makes a country great. But the different levels of government, like the spring fair committees, have to work together, communicate, and co-ordinate their efforts.

Different levels of government are connected to each other. What one level of government decides to do has an impact on the other levels.

What impact do you think these decisions might have on the other levels of government?

- A local government decides that it can no longer afford to give money to community groups for recreation programs for children and teenagers. Many of the programs will have to be cancelled.

- The federal government cuts the amount of money it gives to the provinces for health care.

- A provincial government decides to encourage industrial growth by requiring fewer environmental safeguards.

- The federal government decides to let more people immigrate to Canada each year.

Let's look at the first example. Recreation programs are important for a number of reasons:

- They contribute to good health, self-confidence, friendships, and new skills.

- They offer an inexpensive way to participate in a variety of activities, like crafts, games, and sports.

- Recreation programs provide after-school supervision for children while parents are at work. Being physically active and having fun is a healthier choice than sitting at home watching television alone.

Since physical activity is important for good health, fewer recreation activities may increase the number of illnesses and other health problems in the community. This will raise the cost of health care in the province. Also, when children and young teenagers are left alone with nothing to do, some of them might get into trouble. This will affect the justice system, which involves both provincial and federal levels of government.

When the founders of our country laid out the division of powers and responsibilities between the federal and provincial governments, they thought it was all quite clear. Their vision was a strong federal government with certain powers belonging to the provinces. Their only mention of local government was to say that the provinces were responsible for municipalities. They could not imagine how complicated it would be to govern in the future.

So much has changed since 1867 when Canada came into being as a country:

- Most people now live in urban centres and require many municipal services.

- Because of advances in medical care, people live longer and expect to receive the best medical care available.

- Education through high school, paid for by taxes, is available to all.

- Services like food banks and drop-in centres, often sponsored by churches and community groups, help people in need. But only governments have the resources to provide the social services for those who are homeless, out of work, or struggling to feed their families.

The Hotel Dieu hospital in Kingston.

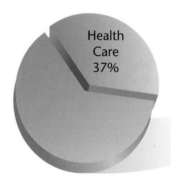

Health Care 37%

In Ontario's budget for 2001, the province planned to spend more than one third of all money on health care.

These are examples of provincial responsibilities that are now immensely important. They are also expensive, and the provinces require financial assistance from the federal government in order to meet them.

The federal government transfers money to the provinces to help pay for the cost of hospital care, doctors' services, education beyond high school, and social programs. It also provides *equalization payments* to provinces that have limited resources. These payments transfer money from wealthier regions to poorer regions so that all of Canada will have adequate health and social services.

In the same way, municipalities require assistance from their provincial governments to provide services. Property taxes alone do not provide enough income for large urban centres to maintain roads, public transportation, emergency services, low-cost housing for families in need, shelters for the homeless, and so on.

If you read the newspaper or listen to the news, it may seem to you that the various levels of government spend too much time arguing rather than communicating, and too little time thinking about how they can co-ordinate their efforts. This is one of the biggest challenges that our governments face: to recognize that they are connected, that the decisions of one level of government have an impact on the other levels, and that they can achieve their goals only by working together for the good of the whole country.

The Trans Canada Trail

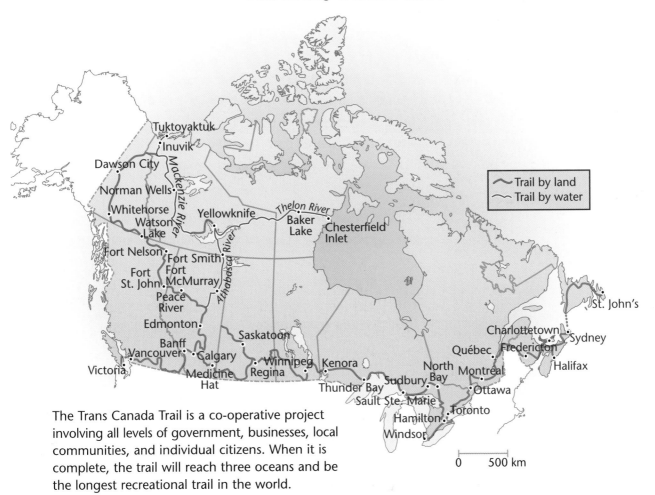

The Trans Canada Trail is a co-operative project involving all levels of government, businesses, local communities, and individual citizens. When it is complete, the trail will reach three oceans and be the longest recreational trail in the world.

LIVING TOGETHER: HEALTH CARE

"Just over 55 years ago, my mother was operated on .... After she had been in hospital for a week, we went to visit her ... and found her crying almost inconsolably. Some idiot ... had left her bill for her surgery and first week on her bedside table. My parents' savings of 22 years were gone."

It's hard to believe that getting sick in Canada was once one of the worst things that could happen. People had to pay all their medical bills, whether they had measles, a broken leg, or were a mother having a baby. Many people suffered terrible hardship.

In 1961, Saskatchewan's premier, Tommy Douglas, established a health-care program for all citizens of his province. Instead of the sick being responsible for paying their own bills, everyone would pay a little bit through taxes so that anyone who needed to see a doctor could do so without worrying about the cost.

Premier Douglas fought long and hard to create a health-care program, and it quickly proved very popular. A program that began in one province ended up having an impact on the whole country. In 1967, the Canadian government established tax-supported health care for all of Canada. Today, most Canadians believe that medicare is our most important social program.

Premier Tommy Douglas

"When we're talking about medical care we're talking about our sense of values. Do we think human life is important? Do we think that the best medical care which is available is something to which people are entitled, by virtue of belonging to a civilized community?"

Being Canadian

Citizens of Canada

"We'd better get going," Ernie said as he helped clean up after dinner. "The polls close at nine."

"Are you coming with us?" his father asked. "I thought you were going with your friends."

"I was going to, but Andy has to work, so he voted after school. And Frank says there's no point," Ernie said.

"No point in voting!" Mrs. Salazar said. "Just imagine if everyone felt that way!"

"Well, he says that the people running for government make all sorts of promises, and then they do exactly what they want," Ernie explained.

"If that's what he thinks, he should do something about it," Mr. Salazar said. "It's all the more reason to vote."

"In all the years since we became Canadian citizens, we have always voted," Mrs. Salazar said. "It's an important responsibility."

"I know, Mami," Ernie said. "You tell Frank the next time you see him."

"I will," she said firmly. "Now, let's go and vote."

Becoming a Canadian

When the Salazar family came to Canada from Mexico ten years ago, they looked forward to becoming citizens. The day they took the oath of citizenship was an important one in their lives.

"From this day forward, I pledge my loyalty and allegiance to Canada and Her Majesty Queen Elizabeth the Second, Queen of Canada. I promise to respect our country's rights and freedoms, to defend our democratic values, to faithfully observe our laws and fulfill my duties and obligations as a Canadian citizen."

Like the Salazars, people from all over the world immigrate to our country. Some are:

- sponsored by family members who are already in Canada. Sponsors promise to provide financial help if it is needed.

- independent immigrants, who are accepted on the basis of their education, job skills, and work experience.

- forced to leave their homeland because of persecution or war, and enter Canada as refugees.

Inspired by Archbishop Oscar Romero of San Salvador, Romero House in Toronto helps refugee families from the time they arrive in Canada until, like this family, they become Canadian citizens.

After three years of living in Canada, immigrants may apply to become citizens. Children under the age of 18 do not have to apply separately, but are included in their parents' application. They receive Canadian citizenship at the same time as their parents.

- The first step is to complete an application form, and send it to the Federal Department of Citizenship and Immigration. Those who meet all the requirements receive a letter telling them where they are to go to take their citizenship test. They are also sent a book about Canada to help them prepare for this test.

- The next step is to take the citizenship test. It includes questions about Canada's history and geography, natural resources, and the rights and responsibilities of citizens. The test may be taken in either of Canada's official languages, French or English. After a few weeks, those who pass receive an important letter, telling them the date and place of their citizenship ceremony.

- The ceremony takes place in a citizenship court. The judge who presides reminds everyone about the rights and responsibilities of Canadian citizens, and then asks the candidates to repeat the oath of citizenship. At the end of the ceremony, each person receives a certificate that shows that he or she is now a full member of the Canadian family.

Immigration to Canada

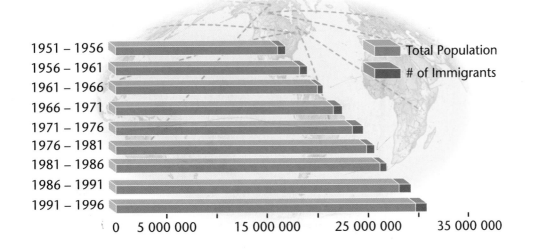

	Total Population
	# of Immigrants

1951 – 1956
1956 – 1961
1961 – 1966
1966 – 1971
1971 – 1976
1976 – 1981
1981 – 1986
1986 – 1991
1991 – 1996

0   5 000 000   15 000 000   25 000 000   35 000 000

LIVING TOGETHER:
THE CHARTER OF RIGHTS

Every country has important dates to celebrate. July 1, 1867, has a special significance for Canadians, for this is the day our country was born.

April 17, 1982, is another big date. Some people describe this as the day that Canada's Constitution came home. Before this time, amendments to our Constitution had to be passed by the British Parliament because the Constitution was a British law. The Constitution Act of 1982 gave Canada the power to amend its own Constitution.

Queen Elizabeth came to Canada to sign the Constitution Act of 1982.

The Constitution Act of 1982 also included for the first time a Canadian Charter of Rights and Freedoms. Some of these rights and freedoms are:

- **democratic rights** — for example, the right to vote and the right to have elections at least every five years

- **fundamental freedoms** — for example, freedom of conscience, religion, and expression

- **mobility rights** — for example, the right to enter or leave Canada, the right to move to another province

- **legal rights** — for example, the right to a fair trial

- **equality rights** — for example, the right to be protected by the law without discrimination based on characteristics such as race, sex, and religion

Over the years we have grown in our understanding of what it means to be citizens of a free and democratic country. There have been times in the past when human rights and freedoms were not respected. For example, at different times both Chinese and Japanese Canadians experienced serious racial discrimination, not just by other citizens, but by the government of Canada. Limitations on the right to vote, based on sex or on what country a person came from, are also part of our history.

It is especially significant that the Charter of Rights and Freedoms is part of our Constitution. Our highest law says that these rights and freedoms must be respected. The Supreme Court, which hears constitutional questions, has the power to decide if some action or law is in conflict with the Charter.

It is important to understand, however, that the rights and freedoms granted by the Charter are not absolute. Governments may pass laws that limit them, as long as these limitations are considered reasonable in a free and democratic society. For example, the right to vote is limited to people who are at least 18 years old. Our right to express ourselves freely is also limited. For example, it is against the law to promote hatred.

As Christians, we believe that each person is created in the image of God, and is called to love and service. Human rights are what we are entitled to in order to fulfill our responsibilities to other people and to God.

Prime Minister Pierre Trudeau was determined to bring the Constitution home and to include the Charter of Rights and Freedoms within it. He believed that Canadians were entitled to this protection: "Our Charter exists to prevent abuses of power by governments or people in positions of authority, so that individuals may find fulfillment in freedom within the civil society."

Responsible Citizens

Citizenship brings both rights and responsibilities. If you read the oath of citizenship on page 52, you will notice it includes a number of promises. These promises are about the responsibilities of being a citizen. Not everyone has the opportunity to take this oath in a citizenship court, but all members of the family of Canada share these responsibilities.

"I promise to respect our country's rights and freedoms."

Our rights and freedoms as Canadians are also responsibilities. When people gather to demonstrate about a situation, they are exercising their freedom of thought, expression, and peaceful assembly. In order to fulfill their responsibilities toward other people, however, they must refrain from violence, and recognize that others have the freedom to disagree with them.

"I promise to defend our democratic values."

Governments are accountable to the people of Canada. But we also have responsibilities if we want our country to be truly democratic. We must take the time to become informed citizens, to vote in elections, and to let our representatives know what we think about the way they are steering the country. A public hearing on proposed legislation is a good opportunity for responsible citizens to make their views known.

"I promise to faithfully observe our laws."

All citizens share the responsibility to obey the laws of Canada. Stopping for pedestrians at crosswalks, respecting the property rights of others, and settling disputes without violence are just a few examples of responsible citizenship. The laws of Canada are intended to protect our rights and freedoms, and to help us live together in a peaceful and just society.

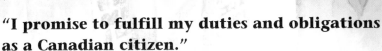

"I promise to fulfill my duties and obligations as a Canadian citizen."

Obeying the laws of Canada, voting, and respecting the rights of others are all important duties of citizens. But being good citizens also means participating in our communities — helping a neighbour, coaching a team, or collecting donations for a charity. As citizens, we have a duty to work together to make our communities and country a good home for everyone. We must also do what we can to serve the people of the world.

The Common Good

There are many gifts, but always the same Spirit. There are many ways of serving, but always the same Lord. There are many activities, but in everybody the same God is at work in them all. The gifts of the Spirit granted to each person are to be used for the common good.

1 Corinthians 12:4-7

The Family of Canada

St. Paul wrote these words almost 2000 years ago in a letter to the Christian community in Corinth. He wanted to remind the people about the kind of life that Christians are called to live.

St. Paul's words are also for us. God creates us out of love, and gives us both gifts and responsibilities. The gifts of intelligence and free choice allow us to understand, to make decisions for ourselves, and to accept responsibility for the way we live.

Scripture also tells us that we are created in the image of God, which means that we are God's representatives in the world. We have been given the responsibility to care for the world, and make it a good home for everyone. The decisions we make about our life together as members of communities and as citizens of Canada are an expression of our faith in Jesus Christ.

To be God's representatives is not a responsibility we can fulfill alone. But we have received another gift — the gift of each other. From the day we are born, we depend on other people in our lives — family members and friends. As we grow up, we continue to discover how deeply we are connected to other people.

We are connected to members of our faith community.

We are connected to the people who live in our neighbourhood.

We are connected to the people with whom we work.

We are connected to the people with whom we share a country.

You already know how important some of these connections are. When you pray together in your classroom or parish church, work as part of a group on a school project, or participate as a member of a neighbourhood team, you know that you are connected. You belong. You are a member of the group and have a contribution to make. When all members of the group contribute their gifts, something wonderful happens. Each person benefits in a special way from being part of the group. The goodness that is created by praying together, working together, or playing together is shared by all. It is a common good.

It is more difficult to recognize and understand our connections as citizens of Canada. There are about 30 million people in our country. You might wonder: How can I be connected to so many people I don't even know?

The simplest way to answer this question is with an image. All human societies are something like families. Members of a family share the responsibility of creating a strong and loving home, and the family accepts responsibility for each of its members. Being a family means sharing resources, showing respect for each other, and being willing to help each other. When one person in a family is ill or upset, the other members provide extra care and attention.

We, the people of Canada, are not just 30 million individuals who happen to live in the northern part of North America. We are members of the Canadian family, and, like a family, we have to make decisions about how we will live together. As members of the Canadian family, each of us benefits from the common good of our society.

As a society we have decided that:

- All members of the Canadian family have rights and freedoms that must be respected and protected.

- No one should be denied medical care because of cost.

- Education is essential, and the expense should be shared by members of the Canadian family.

- People who are unable to work or cannot find work should be able to count on assistance.

- Older people who are no longer working must have sufficient income to meet their basic needs.

- Mothers or fathers should be able to spend some time at home with a new baby without losing their jobs.

All families, including the family of Canada, experience small differences and irritations. Children grumble about fairness or privileges, and parents get upset about undone chores or lack of co-operation. Within our Canadian family, we complain about high taxes or how long it takes for our government to act on important issues.

But if we lose sight of the well-being of the whole family, our differences can become more serious. Instead of working together, we begin to feel resentful and divided. Instead of finding solutions, we find more things to complain about.

This is exactly what happens when we lose sight of the well-being of the whole Canadian family. We start to feel resentful, and overlook what we share in common. We ask:

- "No one helped me, so why should I care about helping others?"

- "I don't have any children, so why should I pay for schools?"

- "Why should I contribute to employment insurance when I've never been unemployed?"

- "What's the point in working hard when the government takes my money and gives it to people who won't work?"

When we ask such questions, we are forgetting that human beings are not all the same. Like members of a family, we have a great variety of gifts and talents. Some of us are blessed with many resources — a strong family, opportunities, and no major worries about money. Or, we may have very limited resources and few opportunities. Some of us are healthy, while others face chronic illnesses or serious disabilities. What happens to us in life depends on luck to some extent.

As Christians, we believe that human beings are more important than their particular gifts or the circumstances of their lives. We are all children of God and should be able to count on each other. The decisions we make about how we will live together must be guided by this belief. Since God never abandons us, how can we abandon each other?

You have probably heard the story of the Good Samaritan. Jesus has just been asked about what a person must do to inherit eternal life. The questioner knows the answer, and, prompted by Jesus, he repeats the great commandment:

"You shall love the Lord your God with all your heart, and with all your soul, and with all your strength, and with all your mind; and your neighbour as yourself."

But then comes another question: "And who is my neighbour?" Jesus responds with the story of the Good Samaritan, the only person who stopped to help a wounded man lying by the roadside. He tended to the man's wounds and arranged for further care.

The Good Samaritan acted as a neighbour, and Jesus tells us that we must "go and do likewise." We have to ask ourselves: "Who are our neighbours?" Are they:

- people who are out of work and need help?
- children who need an education?
- people who cannot participate fully in our society?

If we believe all these people are our neighbours, then they are deserving of our help and concern. They are entitled to a Canadian family that works together to create a society in which people can live with dignity.

The Good Samaritan by Vincent Van Gogh

How difficult is it for Christians to put these beliefs into action? Very difficult — so difficult that it takes a lifelong effort just to overcome our tendency to be more concerned about ourselves than others. But we're not alone in this effort. We have other people in our lives who teach us how to love generously, and we have prayer. The God who creates us never abandons us, and offers us help at every step along the way.

From your experiences as a family member, a friend, and a classmate, you already know the difference you can make. Your contribution to the common good of your family, classroom, school, teams — all of the groups in which you participate — is invaluable. It is also an important preparation for the future when you will take on the challenges of contributing to the common good of your community and your country.

LIVING TOGETHER: TAXES AND THE COMMON GOOD

There are a variety of ways in which we share resources within the family of Canada:

- People contribute time, goods, and money to individuals, community groups, and charities.

- Churches, community organizations, and charitable groups provide assistance and support to those who are most in need of attention within the Canadian family — isolated elderly people, families living in poverty, the homeless, people with serious disabilities, communities that have experienced a natural disaster.

All these activities are a response to the question: "Who is my neighbour?"

During the winter, many churches are part of the Out of the Cold program. Out of the Cold volunteers provide a place to sleep and a meal to people in need.

But individuals and organizations cannot offer social programs and services that take into account the needs of all Canadians. This is a task for our governments. We elect people to represent us, and we also provide the necessary resources through our taxes. No one person can build a hospital or provide assistance to those who are unemployed. But together, we can. By joining forces and each providing a share of the money that is needed, we are contributing to the common good of our Canadian family.

We raise the money that is needed through a variety of taxes, such as income tax, sales tax, and property tax. Income tax is based on a person's ability to pay, and those who have more, pay a higher rate of income tax. This is not the case for sales and property taxes. We all pay at the same rate, no matter what our income.

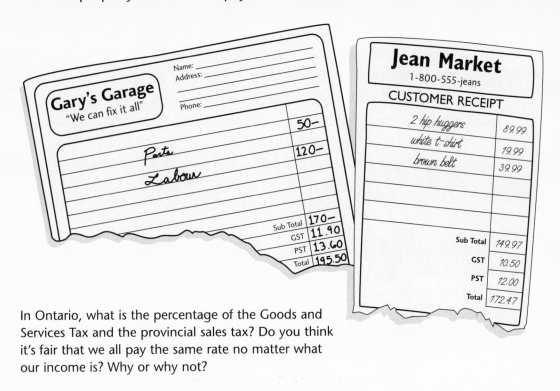

In Ontario, what is the percentage of the Goods and Services Tax and the provincial sales tax? Do you think it's fair that we all pay the same rate no matter what our income is? Why or why not?

Paying our fair share of taxes is an important responsibility. Society cannot work if people do not do their part. As well as everyone paying a fair share, the tax system itself must be fair, with those most able to pay contributing a larger proportion of the money. We also have the right to expect that our governments will be good stewards of the resources we contribute, and make wise decisions about how they are to be used.

Like a family, when we share our resources we can do great things together. Over the years, we have made many good decisions about our common life. In the past, we chose to share our resources to provide education for the young, pensions for senior citizens, and health care for all members of our Canadian family. In the future, there will be new challenges and new decisions to make. The taxes we pay are a visible sign that we are committed to each other and to the common good of our country.

Remembering the Past

For seven years in a row, an annual United Nations report singled out Canada as the best place to live. It is a great honour to be judged the best country in the world in which to live. The United Nations report gives us one more reason to be proud to be Canadians. It is also an important reminder that there is still work to be done to make Canada a good home for all of its citizens.

When a person or group is honoured in some way, the first reaction is often pride. But after pride, comes gratitude. Whether it's winning a sports trophy, receiving a medal in a music competition, or being judged the best place to live, all accomplishments are the result of the participation and efforts of many people. Receiving an award is a special opportunity to remember our connections to other people, and to say thank you.

As Canadians, we have many people to remember and thank.

- When the earliest European settlers came to Canada hundreds of years ago, they would not have survived without the help of the Aboriginal people. Learning how to navigate the lakes and rivers by canoe, to use the hides and fur of animals for clothing and shelter, to recognize plants that supplied necessary vitamins — these are just a few of the skills the Aboriginal people shared with the settlers.

- Long before we became a country in 1867, thousands of pioneer families crossed the Atlantic Ocean and began the backbreaking work of creating a new home. They contributed their farming skills and their knowledge as they cleared the land, planted crops, and built mills, churches, and schools. Dedicated nuns and priests came to serve the pioneers, and establish schools, hospitals, and orphanages. Farms and villages began to dot the landscape. The contributions of Canada's early pioneers and their commitment to this new land laid the foundation of our country.

- The leaders of the colonies in British North America who came together in 1864 had no idea whether it was possible to join together. But they persisted, and three years later Canada became a country.

- In the years after our country's birth, new groups of pioneers began to settle in the west. Work started on a railroad to unite the country from the Atlantic to the Pacific. This almost impossible dream was made possible by an immense army of workers. They laid track across the rocky Canadian Shield and the vast stretches of the Prairies. Thousands of workers came to British Columbia from China to take on the dangerous task of laying track through the peaks and valleys of the mountains. Many of them died in the process.

- Each year, on November 11, we observe Remembrance Day to recall and express our gratitude to Canadians who fought in three wars — World War I, World War II, and the Korean War. Altogether, over 100 000 Canadians, many of them still in their teens, died in these conflicts.

We are connected to all of these people of the past. They are our ancestors in the family of Canada. Whatever we do and accomplish today is built on their dreams, their efforts, and their sacrifices.

Over the years, many people have chosen to serve as our elected representatives. Today, when politicians are so often criticized, it is easy to forget what an important contribution good public servants make. Here are just a few examples of men and women who dedicated their energy and talents to strengthening the family of Canada.

Wilfrid Laurier was the first French-Canadian Prime Minister. His commitment to attracting more settlers to the western region of the country led to half a million immigrants from central and eastern Europe joining the Canadian family.

Wilfrid Laurier
Prime Minister,
1896–1911

Agnes Macphail was the first woman to be elected as a Member of Parliament. She was an outspoken supporter of farmers, and also fought to improve the treatment of people in prison.

Agnes Macphail
Member of Parliament,
1921–1940

Lester Pearson served Canada as Ambassador to the United States, MP, Cabinet Minister, and Prime Minister. He is the first Canadian to win the Nobel Peace Prize, given to him for his role in resolving a conflict over the Suez Canal. He proposed a solution that would be used elsewhere in years to come — a United Nations peacekeeping force.

Lester B. Pearson
Prime Minister,
1963–1968

Jeanne Sauvé was not only the first woman to be elected as an MP from the province of Québec, she was also the first woman to be chosen as Speaker of the House. After serving in the House as an MP, a Cabinet Minister, and as Speaker, she became the first woman Governor General of Canada.

Jeanne Sauvé
Speaker of the
House, 1980–1984;
Governor General,
1984–1989

The well-being of our cities, provinces, and country depends on enthusiastic and committed leaders who seek election for the opportunity to serve. It also depends on responsible citizens who are informed, vote in elections, and participate in the life of their communities.

Creating the Future

A country, like a family, is never finished. Learning to live together and to understand our connections is a process that stretches from the past, through the present, and into the future. There are always new challenges and new decisions.

Sometimes, the challenges we face come from our past. The history of most countries includes decisions that were unjust or events that led to divisions. In Canada, there are two major challenges that have been with us for hundreds of years.

- The Aboriginal people of Canada are looking for a new way of belonging to the family of Canada. After many years of government decisions that have harmed their sense of community, culture, and traditions, they are seeking justice. They point to treaties that were unfair or not honoured and to the terrible poverty of many Native communities. The settlement of Aboriginal land claims and the question of self-government for Native communities are issues that must be resolved in a spirit of justice and respect for the original people of Canada.

When Mathew Coon Come was elected Chief of the Assembly of First Nations in 2000, he said, "The time has come to remove the black eye that Canada has on the treatment of its peoples."

- The early history of our country is in part the story of two European nations — France and Britain — who struggled with each other to control the land and resources of this vast territory we know as Canada. As the country developed, French Canadians became more and more concerned about preserving their heritage and language within the family of Canada. In recent years, some of the people of Québec, where most French Canadians live, have come to believe that the only way to remain a distinctly French society is to separate from the rest of Canada. The division between French and English Canada threatens our unity as a country, and is a serious challenge for present and future governments.

As well as these two serious issues from our past, there are certain characteristics of our country that will always be challenging.

- In area, Canada is the second largest country in the world. Only Russia is larger. But our population is relatively small and is spread out over great distances. Transportation of goods and people is difficult and expensive.

- The various regions of Canada — the western provinces, the central region of Ontario and Québec, the Atlantic provinces, and the far North — have their own history, as well as unique concerns and needs. Balancing these concerns and needs in a way that unites rather than divides the family of Canada is an important responsibility of our federal government.

- Canada's federal system of government, with its division of powers, has worked in the past and will continue to work in the future, but only with wise leadership. Like members of a family, the different levels of government have to work together for the good of all if Canada is to remain strong.

Think for a moment about the leaders of the British colonies who gathered in Prince Edward Island in 1864. They knew about the vastness of the land, and about the concerns of French Canada. They also understood that it would be difficult to balance the powers of the individual colonies and a federal government.

But what would they think about the challenges that we face today?

- Canada is a wealthy nation, but it is also a country with a growing gap between the rich and the poor. The unity and well-being of our Canadian family is threatened when some cannot meet their basic needs and others live in luxury. What can we do to change this unjust situation? How can we meet the challenge of reducing poverty?

- Canada is the only country in the world that is officially multicultural. We take pride in our reputation as a family that respects the many traditions, languages, and customs of its members. What can we do to keep this reputation? How can we continue to meet the challenge of creating a welcoming and respectful society?

- We are not alone in our concerns about the quality of our air, soil, and water, and the state of our natural resources. These are worldwide problems that are threatening our climate, our health, and the future of the people who will live on the earth long after we are gone. What can we do to repair the damage? How can we meet the challenge of being good stewards of the gift of creation?

- We have developed an amazing number of tools, devices, and techniques — computers, satellites, laser surgery, automated industrial equipment. New technologies have changed the way we live, work, maintain our health, and communicate. What can we do to make sure these technologies serve the human family? How can we meet the challenge of using the gift of human intelligence to make the world a good home for everyone?

- The wealthy nations of the world, including Canada, represent 20% of the world's people, but 80% of the world's wealth. The remainder of the human family lives in conditions that make it difficult, and often impossible, to have a decent life. What can we do to share the resources of the world in a more just way? How can we meet the challenge of contributing to the common good of the whole human family?

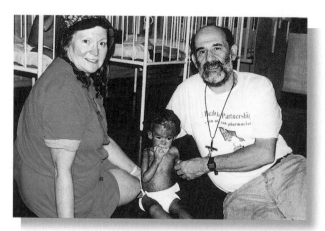

In November 2000, Andrew and Joan Simone received the Order of Canada to honour them for their work as founders of Canadian Food for Children. This is a volunteer organization that collects money and food for starving children around the world.

Earlier you learned about being a member of the family of Canada. We are also members of the world family. The challenge of helping our neighbours at home and throughout the world requires the participation of governments. But our attitudes and actions as individuals also matter. We have to strive to live as disciples of Jesus — recognizing our neighbours in our daily lives, and overcoming our desire to have more than we need. Through prayer, the same Jesus who spoke to his disciples speaks to us, and gives us the strength to meet the challenge of living as sisters and brothers in the family of God.

LIVING TOGETHER: CANADA AND WORLD POVERTY

Canada is a member of the world family of nations. As a member, we have a responsibility to do what we can to improve human life, especially in places where hunger and disease are common.

"God gave the earth to the whole human race for the sustenance of all its members, without excluding or favouring anyone."

As individuals, we can share our resources with those who have the least. We can contribute to organizations that support local projects to help people become more self-sufficient. Some Canadians sponsor a child or family, and send money each month to help with basic needs and education.

These personal responses to poverty make a difference. But the problem is so great that it requires the co-operation of governments around the world to change the circumstances that create poverty. International aid is part of the solution, but only if it reaches the people who need it most, and does not contribute to the burden of debt. Many poor countries owe so much money to wealthy countries that a large proportion of their resources goes to paying their debt.

During the Jubilee year when Christians around the world celebrated the 2000th anniversary of the birth of Christ, 640 000 Canadians signed petitions asking our government to forgive the debt of poor nations. Canada responded by cancelling the debt owed by 11 countries, and calling on other wealthy nations to do likewise. It is a small step on the path to greater justice for the people of the world.

"This is taking a long time!" Carlos complained. "There's a whole bunch of numbers, and a lot of people talking, but they never say who won."

Both Carlos and Rosa had begged to stay up later than usual to watch the election results on television.

"It takes time to count the votes," Mr. Salazar said. "We won't know for a while."

"Our polling station closed just an hour ago," Angie said.

"Imagine what it was like in the past before computers and television," Ernie said. "It must have been a long time before people knew which party was going to form the government."

Rosa sighed. "All I really want to know is who you voted for," she said.

"Well, you won't find that out by watching television," Mrs. Salazar said. "Why don't you both get to bed, and maybe Ernie will tell you in the morning."

"I won't be able to sleep if I don't know," Rosa said.

"I'll probably be awake all night," Carlos added.

"I give up," Ernie said. "You've worn me down!"

The twins cheered, and threw themselves at Ernie. He whispered a name to them, and they went to bed happy.

Lord and Creator
> We thank you for the gift of Canada.
> Help us to make it a good home
> for the whole Canadian family,
> especially those who live in poverty.

Jesus, Son of God
> Teach us to recognize our neighbours,
> and to love them as ourselves.

Spirit of God
> Inspire our leaders to make wise decisions
> for the common good of our country,
> and for the whole human family.
> Fill us with the spirit of generosity and justice.

Amen.

Part II
Early Civilizations

Discovering the Past

Signs of the Past

Have you ever looked at a map of the world and imagined yourself riding on a camel in the deserts of Egypt? Exploring the rain forest in Peru? Visiting the Great Wall of China? What else might you like to do?

Some people are fascinated by a different kind of journey — not to another place, but to another time. "The past is a foreign country," someone once wrote, and it is this country they want to explore.

In some places, the past is visible — ruins of buildings and ancient cities, or pyramids, monuments, and statues that still stand. There is also much hidden deep in the earth. For hundreds of years, often by accident, people have come upon buried evidence of the past — old coins, ancient tools, or a piece of a pot made thousands of years ago.

Locating, identifying, and explaining these treasures of human history is the special field of archaeology. *Archaeology* is the scientific study of people of the past through the materials they left behind, such as buildings, pottery, tools, paintings, tombs, jewellery, and sculptures. Scholars from other fields, like geology, anthropology, and art history also help us understand how people lived and worked together in the country of the past.

Canadian archaelogists at work at a site in Newfoundland.

The Great Zimbabwe

More than 100 years ago, Karl Mauch, a geologist working in Africa, came upon a structure unlike anything he had ever seen before. Covered by the bush and trees of the jungle was the ruin of a great temple, surrounded by a massive circular stone wall over 10 m high and 5 m thick.

The majestic and awe-inspiring Great Zimbabwe is still a mystery that archaeologists are trying to solve. Some think it may have been the residence of the king, his family, and royal courtiers. Others think it may have been a school. Still others think it was the place where important religious rituals were held. As scientific and archaeological work continues, the puzzle of the Great Zimbabwe may one day be solved.

The structure was so extraordinary that Mauch thought he had come upon a copy of King Solomon's Temple or the palace of the Queen of Sheba. Archaeologists who followed him were excited by this possibility.

But they were wrong. Mauch had found the Great Zimbabwe, the most splendid and important structure built in southern Africa before modern times — part of the great Monomotapa Kingdom. In its day, this kingdom controlled a vast territory and had grown rich and powerful by trading gold and ivory for cotton from India and silk from China.

The wall surrounding the Great Zimbabwe is around 300 m long. It is made from 15 000 t of granite cut into almost one million blocks, skilfully put together without any mortar. The wall slopes gently inward to give it stability.

Archaeologists studying the Great Zimbabwe today face problems caused by mistakes of early archaeologists. Materials that did not fit with the idea that the structure might be related to King Solomon's Temple were often ignored or discarded. Also, some objects were taken and sold by treasure hunters. But in recent years, archaeologists have found tools for smelting gold, instruments for making beautiful jewellery, and imported goods from India and China.

China's Clay Soldiers

One spring day in 1974, a group of Chinese farmers started digging a well near the city of Xi'an. They had dug only about four metres when their tools clanked against something unusual.

They stopped work right away and reported what had happened. Archaeologists came to have a look, as one of the most amazing finds of all time was uncovered. In underground vaults, they found row after row of life-size clay figures — archers, foot soldiers, charioteers, and horsemen, all with their weapons and horses. Ten thousand soldiers stood guarding the tomb of the first emperor of China, Shi Huangdi, just as they had been doing for more than 2000 years. It is thought that at least 5000 more remain buried.

The clay soldiers look so lifelike that archaeologists thought that real soldiers must have posed for portraits. Scientists know now that at least eight standard moulds were used for heads, and other moulds for lips, eyes, noses, hair, moustaches and beards. Artists mixed and matched the pieces and also modified the parts to create each individual soldier.

CENTRAL AMERICA
Copán

The Mayan City of Copán

One day in 1838, while visiting a bookstore in New York, John Stephens was shown an obscure book about mysterious ruins in Central America. Stephens, who loved history and travel, was fascinated and became determined to see these sights. A year later he and his friend Frederick Catherwood landed in Central America and set off through the jungles of Belize with a guide, not exactly sure what they were looking for.

Finally, they stood before a massive wall covered with vines, flowers, and other jungle growth. On the other side of the wall were the remains of a city — the long-lost city of Copán. They saw the ruins of huge stone buildings, a pyramid, a theatre, staircases, and strange stone slabs, called *steles*. The steles were covered with intricate carvings and mysterious symbols, called *hieroglyphics*, that they could not read.

The ancient and almost-forgotten civilization of the Maya had been uncovered.

Frederick Catherwood was an artist who painted many of the amazing things he and John Stephens discovered. The work of Catherwood and other early artists and photographers is now very important for scientists because many Mayan monuments have been damaged by weather and people.

The Maya loved to play a ball game called *pok-a-tok*. We don't know all the rules of the game, but we do know that the ball was larger than a basketball, made of solid, heavy rubber, and was very bouncy. Players were not allowed to touch the ball with their hands, but could use only their hips, knees, elbows, or forearms. Without letting the ball touch the ground, players had to get the ball through stone rings attached to the sides of the ball court. The game was taken very seriously. Losing players sometimes lost their lives as well as the game! These photos show the ball court at Chichen Itza, Mexico.

This picture shows a small Mayan statue of a pok-a-tok ballplayer in action. The rubber ball was so hard that players protected themselves by wearing helmets and gloves, and padding on their arms, knees, and hips. The protective belt around the waist was made of wood and animal hide.

Ancient Troy

Like millions before him, Heinrich Schliemann grew up hearing and loving stories about the most famous war in history — the Trojan War.

But unlike almost everyone before him, young Heinrich believed that the stories recounted in the *Iliad* and the *Odyssey* — the kidnapping of beautiful Helen, the anger of brave Achilles, the strategies of clever Odysseus, the death of noble Hector, and the Trojan Horse — were not just exciting legends but had really happened. When he was 14, Heinrich told a friend that one day he would find the place where all these events had occurred — the ancient city of Troy.

The Trojan War lasted for 10 long years, and ended only when the Greek general Odysseus came up with a plan. The Greeks pretended to give up and sail home and left a giant, hollow wooden horse outside the walls of Troy as an offering to the goddess Athena. The happy Trojans brought the horse inside the city, and that night, when the city was asleep, the best Greek warriors emerged from their hiding place inside the horse. They opened the city gates for the Greek army, which had only sailed a short distance away and returned quietly to Troy after dark. After a fierce fight, the Greeks captured Troy and the terrible war was finally over.

Schliemann made a fortune in business, which soon allowed him to spend all his time and money looking for Troy. Even though people laughed at him, he never doubted his dream of finding the ancient city he had read about as a boy. In 1869, he went to a place in Turkey that fit a description in the *Iliad* and started digging. He had almost instant success. In fact, there were nine buried cities on top of each other in that spot! But which was Troy?

When he discovered a collection of breathtaking gold jewellery, Schliemann was sure he had discovered the treasure of King Priam of Troy. Archaeologists today believe he was wrong about the treasure and which city was the real Troy, but Heinrich Schliemann had found Troy and proved to the world there was real history behind Homer's amazing stories.

After finding Troy, Heinrich Schlieman set out to find the ancient Greek kingdom of Mycenae, whose great king, Agamemnon, had led the Greek army to Troy. Once again Schliemann was successful. In the royal tombs he found this gold mask, which he thought was the death mask of Agamemnon himself.

Charting the Past

There are hundreds of amazing stories of archaeological discoveries. Some, like the clay soldiers in China, are wonderful accidents. Others, like the Great Zimbabwe and the Mayan city of Copán, took place during the 19th century when ancient civilizations held a special fascination. People with a love of travel and adventure hoped to be the first to make an important discovery. Often, they were inspired by vague stories of hidden sites and treasures, and were willing to take a chance that these stories might just be true.

Today, archaeologists are still inspired by the possibility of new discoveries and a better understanding of how ancient people lived. But they no longer rely on stories of hidden treasures. Now they use modern scientific methods to help them in their work.

Photography — Photographs taken from the air allow archaeologists to locate promising new sites, and also to discover important details about sites that are already being explored. A bird's-eye view provides information not visible from the ground.

Underwater photography also allows archaelogists to see and study scientific evidence of places and objects that have been lost and forgotten for hundreds and even thousands of years.

Scientists working at an underwater site off the coast of Turkey survey a section of a long-lost sunken ship.

Carbon-dating — The science of physics gave archaeologists an important tool for establishing the age of objects. All living things absorb a type of radioactive carbon from the environment, called *carbon-14*. When a plant or animal dies, carbon-14 begins to decay at a constant rate. By measuring the level of carbon-14 that remains, it is possible to determine how old an object is. This method can be used on anything that came from something that was once alive, such as wood, bone, charcoal, shells, leather, and paper.

Excavation techniques — When archaeologists begin to excavate, they follow very careful procedures to preserve the evidence they find. Sometimes, a single deep trench is dug to expose the layers beneath the earth's surface. Most ancient ruins are made up of layers, each representing a different time period. The oldest layer, where the first village was built, is the deepest layer. If the site was inhabited for hundreds or thousands of years, there will be evidence of newer structures built on top of older ones.

This photograph shows a working site in the ancient African city of Meroe discovered in present-day Sudan. What do you think the red and white coloured pole is for?

Then each layer is explored. Archaeologists make careful records of where items are found. Uncovering and documenting an important site requires years of painstaking work. Even then, there will likely be areas left unexplored, and questions left unanswered.

Africa Nubia and the Kush	The Americas The Maya
3500 B.C – 3000 B.C.	
• hieroglyphics in Egypt • early settlement in Nubia • Egypt unites	• corn is cultivated in mesoamerica
3000 B.C. – 2500 B.C.	
• Great Pyramid at Giza • Kerma settlement	
2500 B.C. – 2000 B.C.	
• Egypt conquers Lower Nubia	
2000 B.C. – 1500 B.C.	
1500 B.C. – 1000 B.C.	
• Egypt destroys Kerma • King Tutankhamen buried	• Olmec people
1000 B.C. – 500 B.C.	
• Kingdom of Kush • Kush conquers Egypt • Taharqo rules Egypt and Kush	• early Maya settlements
500 B.C. – 0	
• Nok people • Heroditus visits Nubia • Queen of Kush fights Rome	• first Maya cities built • Maya invent "zero" • pok-a-tok first played
0 – 500 A.D.	
• Egypt becomes a Roman province • Last king of Kush is buried • Kingdom of Axum	• first inscribed stele • Teotihuacan founded
500 A.D. – 1000 A.D.	
• Islamic Empire at its height • Kingdom of Ghana	• King Pacal of Palenque • King Au Cacau • Toltec people
1000 A.D. – 1500 A.D.	
• The Great Zimbabwe • Kingdom of Mali • Kingdom of Benin	• Mayapan founded • Chichen Itza abandoned • Aztec Empires • Christopher Columbus reaches the Americas

Asia The Han Chinese	Europe and the Middle East The Romans
• farming communities on the Yellow River	• Sumerian people • invention of writing in Mesopotamia • invention of the wheel
• Indus people in India	
	• Minoan people on Crete
• Shang dynasty • silk weaving in China • first writing in China	• Hammurabi's Law Code • Assyrian people
• Zhou dynasty	• Trojan War
• Hindus invent "zero" • Siddhartha (Buddha) born in India • Confucius born	• Phoenician alphabet • First Olympic Games • Rome founded • Nebuchadnezzar rules Babylon
• cast-iron used in China • Mauryan empire in India • Qin dynasty • Great Wall of China • Han dynasty begins	• Athenian democracy • Celts invade Rome • Alexander the Great • first Roman aqueduct built • Hannibal fights Rome
• invention of paper in China • invention of the wheelbarrow • Silk Road • Han dynasty ends	• Jesus is born • Mount Vesuvius erupts • Emperor Marcus Aurelius • Emperor Constantine becomes a Christian • Last Western emperor deposed
• Sui dynasty reunites China • Tang dynasty begins	• Emperor Justinian's Law Code • Vikings settle in Canada
• Ming dynasty begins	• Normans invade England • John Cabot sets sail

Understanding Civilization

Hunters of the Stone Age

Prehistoric works of art have been found all around the world. Some of these creations are more than 30 000 years old. We use the word *prehistoric* to describe them because they come from a period of time before there are any written records of human history. This painting of a bison was found in a cave at Altamira, Spain.

Who are the ancient people who decorated the walls of their rocky shelters with pictures of deer, bison, horses, and other animals? What do we know about them? How did they live?

The period of time from about 40 000 years ago until about 12 000 years ago is the last part of the *Stone Age* or *Paleolithic* period. *Paleolithic* comes from two Greek words meaning *old* and *stone*. The names for this period refer to the stone tools that prehistoric people made and used.

From studies of the way people lived during the last part of the Stone Age, we know that they:

- moved from place to place, following the animals they needed for food.

- used caves for shelter, or, if there were no caves, built tents and huts, or dug pits for temporary homes.

- used fire for heat and cooking.

- made tools using natural materials — stones, wood, and animal bones.

- used animal skins for clothing and shelter.

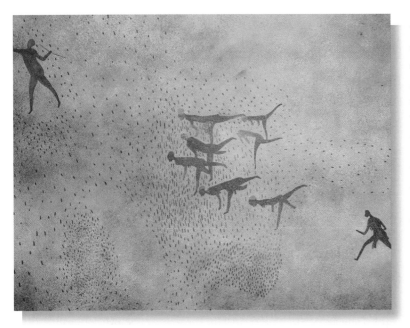

This prehistoric rock painting was found in the Sahara region of Africa, and is probably about 5000 years old. It was created during a time when the desert was a fertile region with rivers and valleys, and many fish and animals. Climate change caused the Sahara to dry up around 4000 years ago. The scene in this painting — women gathering wild grain — has been compared to a graceful ballet dance.

Perhaps people of the Stone Age stayed in the same location when they found a place with lots of edible plants and animals. It was likely during one of these times that they felt the urge to create a record of their lives on the walls and ceiling deep inside the cave. They made paints from crushed rocks and plants. Their art mainly represents what they knew — the hunt for animals on which their lives depended.

Most scholars think these paintings have a magical or religious meaning. Did prehistoric people believe they could ensure a successful hunt by creating animal images? Or did they want to show their appreciation to the unknown spirits that controlled the herds?

The answers to these questions are buried in the past. But we can look at pictures of the cave paintings, and be sure of one thing — we are in the presence of human intelligence and creativity.

IN THE IMAGE OF GOD:
INTELLIGENT AND CREATIVE
SEEKING BEAUTY

From the earliest prehistoric cave paintings right up to our own time, people have used their creativity to beautify their world and their lives. Because most artwork is fragile, little survives from ancient days except things that were made from hard substances like stone or metal. Here are a few beautiful objects crafted by our ancestors.

Sculpture is a very important part of the artistic tradition of Africa. This bronze plaque from the Kingdom of Benin shows two royal soldiers.

The Celts loved to make intricate patterned metalwork. This cup has been decorated with gold in a swirling pattern. Celts often based their designs on the circle and other geometric forms.

After the Celts of Ireland became Christian, they used some of their favourite design ideas in their beautiful manuscript copies of the Gospels and their carvings of large stone crosses.

Some of the largest wooden sculptures ever carved are the totem poles created by the Aboriginal peoples of Canada's west coast. Totem poles were made from red cedar, whose wood is firm and durable but easy to cut.

Totem poles told family stories and legends, and involved animals like ravens, wolves, and thunderbirds.

Religious faith has inspired artists in all civilizations. This bronze image shows Shiva, one of the Hindu gods of India, as Lord of the Dance.

One of the most amazing archaeological events of all time was the discovery in 1922 of the tomb of the ancient Egyptian pharaoh, Tutankhamun. This mask had been placed over the head of his mummy. It is made of solid gold and the eyebrows and eyelashes of lapis lazuli, a precious stone.

Early Agriculture

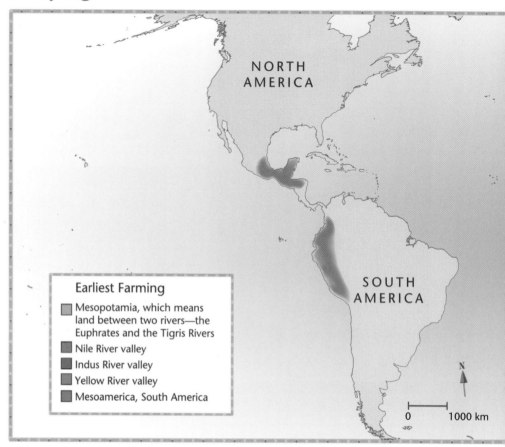

Earliest Farming
- Mesopotamia, which means land between two rivers—the Euphrates and the Tigris Rivers
- Nile River valley
- Indus River valley
- Yellow River valley
- Mesoamerica, South America

About 10 000 B.C.*, as the last Ice Age came to an end, the climate began to warm. People could now live in areas that had once been covered with sheets of ice. Not long after, about 9000 B.C., something so momentous happened that it can truly be called a revolution. Over several thousand years, and in different locations around the world, farming began. People began to grow their own plants and raise the animals they needed.

You might wonder — what is so revolutionary about farming?

---

*In many western cultures dates are calculated and written in relation to the birth of Christ. For example, the year 1000 B.C. is one thousand years before the birth of Christ. B.C. stands for "Before Christ." The year 1000 A.D. is one thousand years after the birth of Christ. A.D. stands for "Anno Domini," which is Latin for "year of the Lord."

Some people use BCE in place of B.C., and C.E. in place of A.D.. B.C.E. stands for Before the Common Era. With this system, the year 1000 B.C.E. is one thousand years before the birth of Christ. C.E. stands for Common Era. The year 1000 C.E. is one thousand years after the birth of Christ.

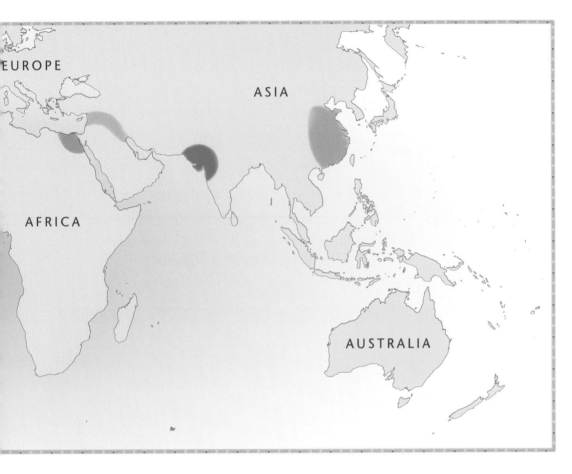

Imagine a world in which the most basic need of all — food — could only be met by constant travel. As animal herds roamed over the land, humans followed. They found or made rough shelters, and enriched their diet with edible plants. But the idea of settling down and having greater control over their lives was unimaginable — until the beginning of farming.

No one knows just how it began. It seems likely that some repeated experience gradually led people to realize they could be food producers instead of food gatherers. Perhaps, when they returned to a place where they had once stayed, they noticed a heavy growth of plants in an area where they had prepared and eaten their food. Did they connect this new growth with the many seeds that would have fallen on the ground? We don't know.

In the same way, hunters began to control the herds they followed. Eventually, people kept animals on farms for a reliable source of food.

Agriculture was the first step in an amazing journey — the development of human civilization. In areas where there was farming, small villages grew up. Because people remained in one place to care for their crops and animals, they built permanent homes. They also began to create useful items like furniture and containers for food. Over time, new materials and skills were discovered, such as making copper tools and creating pottery from clay.

As villages grew into towns, not everybody had to be directly involved with food production. The fields that surrounded the settlement could support other activities — metal working, making clay bricks and pottery, and other crafts. In exchange for the items people made, they received the food they needed.

These are ruins from the walls of Jericho, the oldest known town in the world. Jericho, which is near Jerusalem, was first inhabited around 7000 B.C.

Look back at the map on pages 96–97. In these areas of the world, and over several thousand years, a complex and organized way of life developed from simple farming communities. Villages became towns, some towns grew into magnificent centres, and several great human civilizations were born.

Marks of Civilization

If someone asked you, "What is a school?", you might answer, "a place where people learn." But learning also occurs in other settings, such as homes, playgrounds, or workplaces. To explain how schools are different, you would have to be more specific. What are the main characteristics of schools that set them apart from other places?

To explain a civilization, we have to ask the same kind of question: What are the main characteristics of a civilization that set it apart from other types of human communities? It is not an easy question to answer, and scholars have differing opinions.

Let's begin our answer with a brief journey to the region of the world where civilization first appeared around 3000 B.C. — Mesopotamia. The year is 570 B.C., and the place is Babylon, where King Nebuchadnezzar is the all-powerful ruler.

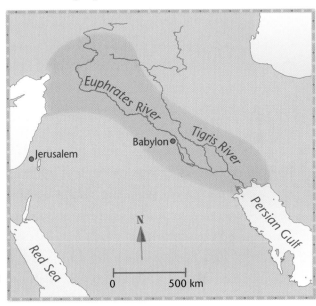

This map shows the empire of Babylon at the time of King Nebuchadnezzar.

For Christians and Jews, Nebuchadnezzar is known as the fierce warrior-king who exiled the people of Israel to Babylon in 586 B.C. This painful event is described in Scripture:

> *By the rivers of Babylon we sat down;*
> *there we wept when we remembered Zion.*
> *On the willows nearby we hung our harps.*
> *How can we sing the Lord's song in a foreign land?*
>
> *Psalm 137:1,2,4*

But Nebuchadnezzar is also famous as the ruler who made his city one of the most beautiful in history.

KING NEBUCHADNEZZAR'S BABYLON

The two bodyguards had sat through the night outside the royal chambers, and were half asleep when the steward arrived with the king's breakfast — grilled fish, flat barley bread with date syrup, grapes, and beer. They both said a silent prayer to the great god Marduk that the steward would not mention their sleepiness to the king.

Once his body was bathed and anointed with sesame oil and perfumes, King Nebuchadnezzar was ready to begin the day. As he ate his meal, two officials from the Temple of Esagila arrived to give him the latest news. Both had recently returned from highly successful trade missions. New shipments of cedar, stone, olive oil, and precious metals had been arranged. The amount of grain and wool the officials had agreed to pay for these shipments could easily be supplied.

After this meeting, the king left the palace to begin his favourite part of the day — an inspection of his beloved city. Several of his soldiers rode in his chariot with him — men with whom he had fought side by side in many battles.

As always, the morning tour began down the Processional Way to the Temple of Esagila. It was along this wide road that the king and high priests processed each year with the image of Marduk, the greatest of the Babylonian gods. It seemed as if all 200 000 people living in the city of Babylon came to watch this procession.

The soldiers remained in the courtyard, and the king entered the temple chapel alone. What a sight it was! To show his great piety, he had ordered that the walls, ceiling, and even the rafters be covered with gold. At one end stood golden images of Marduk and his wife Sarpanitum. Nebuchadnezzar offered a prayer for his kingdom and for victory over all his enemies.

Just north of the Temple of Esagila stood the great *ziggurat* of Babylon. It was almost 90 m high, and at the top was a small temple. The king noted with approval that the repairs done earlier in his reign showed no signs of wear. The bricks that lay over the clay and formed the outer surface had been well made and carefully placed. In the king's opinion, there were no better artisans than those of Babylon.

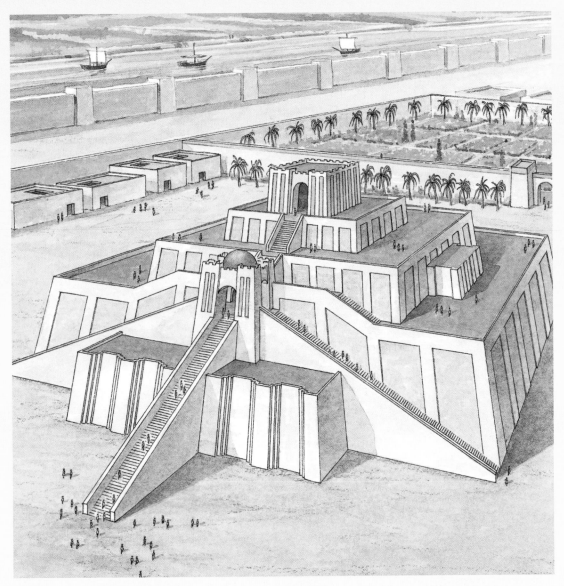

Some people believe that the great ziggurat of Babylon was the Tower of Babel told about in scripture (Genesis 11: 1-9).

Nebuchadnezzar and his soldiers then crossed the wide bridge over the Euphrates River, rode through the newer part of Babylon, and past the outer walls of the city. Before them lay fields of barley and wheat, and pastures with large flocks of sheep and herds of goats. Canals — some of them hundreds of years old — crossed the land, bringing water from the river. Clearing these canals of the silt that built up required large numbers of slaves and hired labourers.

Nebuchadnezzar ended his tour by re-entering the city from the north through the Ishtar Gate. The great high walls leading up to the gate were decorated with rows of ferocious lions made of coloured enamel tiles. The gate itself was decorated with figures of bulls and dragons.

Ishtar was the Babylonian goddess of love, and the king had ordered a magnificent gate built to honour her. This project required thousands of labourers and many skilled artisans. This photograph shows one of the bulls that decorated the Ishtar Gate.

Nebuchadnezzar spent the afternoon on matters related to his kingdom — a legal dispute over land; the state of the army; a report of an attack on a trade caravan; a meeting with the chief priest, who gave his latest predictions for the king's fortune based on the position of the stars. Other officials reviewed the wealth of the kingdom. They read from clay tablets on which business affairs were recorded — weights of wheat and barley, stores of gold, silver, and copper, amounts of raw wool and woolen cloth, and numbers of slaves.

After an evening meal, the king ended the day with his wife, Amyns, in the Hanging Gardens. Nebuchadnezzar had many wives, but it was for Amyns that he had ordered this magnificent terraced building to be created. It was surrounded by a moat, and had pumps that raised water from deep wells to a reservoir at the top. Rich soil was placed on the terraces, and the water from the reservoir nourished a collection of thousands of flowers, ferns, vines, and trees at each level.

Night was falling, and servants lit the oil lamps that surrounded the gardens. The rich perfume of flowers filled the air. Nebuchadnezzar and Amyns sat together, talking quietly. The day had come to an end.

Babylon was a magnificent city, and we know from written records that Nebuchadnezzar took great pride in it. The Hanging Gardens were considered one of the seven wonders of the ancient world. But during your brief visit there was, in fact, more to see than golden chapels, beautiful gardens, roads, and gates. Some of the distinctive characteristics of civilizations were also on display.

As you explore these characteristics in Africa, the Americas, Asia, and Europe, here is something important to remember:

> The development of a civilization is a uniquely human achievement. What distinguishes human beings is the remarkable capacity of our minds. We are seekers of knowledge, and we are users of knowledge. We can reason, learn, plan, solve problems, imagine, and create.

Today, most scholars agree that cities, like Babylon, are a special mark of a civilization. But there are also other important characteristics to consider.

Economic System — In a complex society, or civilization, people specialize in different types of work. In Babylon, you saw some evidence of this specialization:

- Nebuchadnezzar and his officials governed society and planned for the future. They also maintained temples and led religious ceremonies.

- The Babylonians produced, stored, and distributed food. They also traded to obtain items they wanted.

- Labourers and artisans were available for major building projects, and also maintained walls, canals, and temples.

- Some people were responsible for gathering and recording important information.

- A trained army protected the empire from enemies.

The Babylonians, like other ancient civilizations, were able to produce extra food, called a *surplus*. This is an essential achievement for a civilization. With a food surplus, not everyone has to be involved in farming. Some people can work as artisans, builders, soldiers, and government and religious leaders, and receive food in exchange for their services. Also, without a surplus, natural disasters like a long drought or sudden flood could seriously harm or even destroy a community.

A surplus of food or another resource can also be traded. Babylon did not have much stone and wood, but did have extra grain and wool, as well as skilled weavers who created woolen cloth. Trading allows a society to acquire natural resources and goods that improve the quality of life.

The most famous traders of the ancient world from about 1200 B.C. to 300 B.C. were the Phoenicians, who lived along the eastern coast of the Mediterranean Sea. They were excellent shipbuilders, and their sturdy trading ships carried goods all around the Mediterranean.

Social and political system — Over thousands of years, as some farming settlements grew into larger communities, people needed new ways to arrange their life together. An important mark of a civilization is a complex social system that allows people to live together and make decisions.

Although early civilizations differ in many ways, they share one characteristic: their social and political organization was *hierarchical*. A hierarchy places people in ranks, from the highest to the lowest.

A Hierarchical Society

You may have noticed some of these ranks in Babylon. At the top was Nebuchadnezzar, and it was his responsibility to ensure that his empire's needs were met:

- irrigation of fields to produce a food surplus
- trade arrangements to obtain resources and goods
- protection from enemies
- construction of public buildings, walls, and roads
- laws to protect property and people

Trusted officials helped him accomplish these tasks.

A complex society also needs a system for obtaining contributions from its people in the form of labour, military service, and taxes. Without the skilled artisans who made the coloured tiles of the Ishtar gates, the farmers who tended the fields, the soldiers who defended the empire, and the labourers who cleared the canals and built bridges and walls, the civilization of Babylon would not have existed.

IN THE IMAGE OF GOD: INTELLIGENT AND CREATIVE

HONOURING GODS AND RULERS

The complex social and political organization of early civilizations led to some amazing accomplishments. Among these is the creation of some of the most magnificent structures the world has ever known. Imagination, a love of beauty, a desire to display power or religious devotion, the skill and labour of countless people — all are present in these structures. Here are just two examples.

In 1250 B.C., to celebrate the 30th year of his reign and show his power and glory, Egyptian Pharaoh Rameses the Great ordered a magnificent temple to be built at Abu Simbel.

The temple was carved into cliffs rising above the banks of the Nile and its entrance was guarded by four giant seated figures of Rameses himself. Each figure was over 20 m high and weighed over 1000 t. Egyptian engineers designed the temple so that on Rameses' birthday and on the anniversary of his coronation, the morning rays of the sun would fill the whole length of the temple and light up a statue of Rameses at the back.

The entrance to the temple of Rameses the Great. Compare the size of the person at the entrance to the figures of Rameses.

Athena, goddess of wisdom and the arts, was the patron of Athens, the greatest city in Greece. To mark a victory over the Persians in 427 B.C., the Athenians decided to honour her by building a temple — the Parthenon, perhaps the most famous building of the ancient world.

The Parthenon's structure was simple, following the Greek design principles of proportion, harmony, and balance. Its straight lines, however, are an optical illusion. Since a column with perfectly straight lines would look thinner in the middle, the Parthenon's columns were given a slight bulge. The columns also lean in slightly, and the base of the temple roof was raised in the middle so it wouldn't appear to be sagging. In fact, there's hardly a straight line in the whole structure.

The architects used a type of construction called *post-and-lintel*. Vertical columns (posts) hold up horizontal blocks (lintels). With this system, the force of the load travels down to the building's supporting foundations.

Since Athens is in an earthquake zone, the builders cut slots in marble blocks next to each other into which molten lead was poured. When the lead hardened, the blocks held together firmly even without cement.

The Athenians used over 22 000 t of white marble to build the Parthenon. The iron in the marble gives the building a golden glow. The centrepiece of the temple was a statue of Athena, over 12 m high, and adorned with more than a tonne of gold.

Knowledge and technology — In Babylon, as in other ancient civilizations, mathematics was important. Think of the problems they had to solve: How much surplus grain and wool is available for trade? What amount of grain does a farming family owe in taxes? What weight of gold is needed to make a bracelet?

The science of astronomy also developed early. Certain people, most often religious leaders, became skilled in observing the stars, the cycles of the moon, and the changing position of the sun. Based on these observations, they developed calendars to regulate the farming year and the timing of religious celebrations. In Babylon, as in other early civilizations, the position of the moon or planets was also used by priests to predict the future.

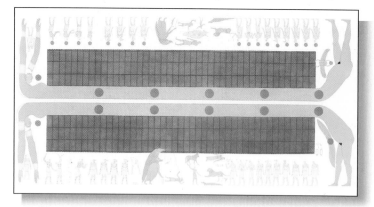

This astronomical table was painted on the ceiling in an Egyptian pyramid.

Ancient people developed many specialized techniques for processing resources and producing goods. In Babylon, there were weavers, masons, goldsmiths, boat builders, shoemakers, bakers, brick makers, brewers, carpenters, millers, and more. Skilled artisans were important in all ancient civilizations.

But the most remarkable ancient technology of all is one that you use every day — writing. A method of recording information in written form came about for a very practical reason: to keep accurate accounts of the food surplus. In Babylon, as you saw, the king's officials relied on records written on clay tablets. Of course, this new technology was so powerful that it came to be used for many purposes: sending messages, recording history, listing laws, preserving myths and legends, and exploring ideas and human experiences.

Like agriculture, writing transformed human society. People no longer had to be in the same place to communicate, but could send messages and letters. Also, their thoughts and experiences could be saved and read by people hundreds, and even thousands, of years later.

HOW EARLY WRITING DEVELOPED

The earliest system of writing developed in Mesopotamia about 3000 B.C., and is known as *cuneiform*, which comes from a Latin word meaning *wedge*. The end of a reed was cut in the shape of a triangle, and wedge-shaped marks were drawn on wet clay tablets.

The Egyptians developed another system of writing called *hieroglyphics*, which comes from a Greek word meaning "sacred writing in stone." The Egyptians wrote on stone and on paper made from papyrus plants.

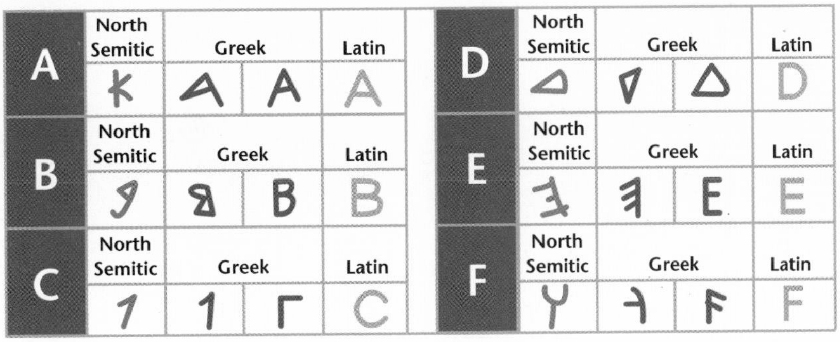

A	North Semitic	Greek		Latin	D	North Semitic	Greek		Latin
A	K	�441	A	A	D	◿	▽	△	D

B	North Semitic	Greek		Latin	E	North Semitic	Greek		Latin
B	𝟫	𝟫	B	B	E	⇃	⇃	E	E

C	North Semitic	Greek		Latin	F	North Semitic	Greek		Latin
C	𝟏	𝟏	Γ	C	F	Y	⅂	F	F

The most recent stage in writing is the use of an alphabet. The first known alphabet, called the North Semitic, developed around 1700 B.C. in the Middle East. It had 22 letters.

Religious beliefs — In an ancient religious text from Mesopotamia, a person who has suffered many setbacks asks: *Who can know the will of the gods in heaven?*

From the beginning, people have asked this kind of question. How did the universe come to be? What powers govern it? What determines the fate of humans? Why is there suffering and pain? What happens to people after death?

The Book of Job in the Old Testament tells the story of Job, a just and good man, who has done no wrong, but has suffered greatly. Job has many questions about his fate, but his faith in God remains steadfast.

Because ancient people were so dependent on the natural world — the fertility of the soil, the warmth of the sun, the moisture of the rains, the annual flooding of rivers — they came to believe that nature was controlled by spirits or gods. Over time, this belief in powerful spirits included other aspects of life, such as gods who determined the outcome of war or childbirth and gods who protected individual towns and cities. People developed rituals to communicate with these powerful spirits. They also built monumental structures, like the Parthenon, to honour their gods.

Early Mesopotamian people believed their gods wanted them to live honest lives, respect the law, and pray constantly. Because it wasn't possible to pray all the time, they came up with the idea of creating praying statues to take their place. This photograph shows a typical praying stone statue, with large, intense eyes and hands folded in prayer. These statues were placed in front of the altars of the gods and left there permanently.

The names of gods and the way people worshipped differed from place to place. But the role of religion is similar in all ancient civilizations:

- Religious beliefs brought people together and helped create a united and orderly society.

- Rulers and religious leaders were believed to have a special connection to the gods that gave them the authority to govern.

- All ancient people struggled with the question of what happens after death. They arrived at different answers, but for all of them there was a sense that some part of the person survived.

The quest to understand the world and ourselves continues today. Science can explain many matters that were mysterious to ancient peoples, but the deep longings of the human spirit remain — to believe in something beyond oneself, and to seek a purpose and meaning in life.

The Past in Africa

AFRICA

The Gift of the Nile

The Nile is the longest river in the world, flowing 6671 km from central Africa all the way to the Mediterranean Sea. On either side of the river are deserts: the Sahara to the west, and the Arabian and Nubian deserts to the east. But between these deserts lies the fertile valley of the Nile.

The Nile Valley in Modern Times

The source of the Nile River lies deep in the heart of Africa, near Lake Victoria. The source of the Blue Nile, which joins the main river at Khartoum, lies in the mountains of Ethiopia.

The Nile Valley in Ancient Times

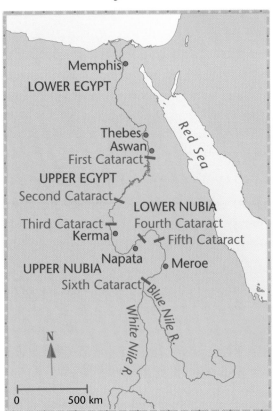

Let's begin a journey at the mouth of the Nile where it empties into the Mediterranean Sea, and travel upriver to Khartoum:

- The Nile has the largest delta in the world. A *delta* is an area at the mouth of a river where earth and bits of rock have been deposited. Over time, this sediment creates an area with channels and small islands. This region of the Nile was very fertile in ancient times.

- Just south of Aswan, the soft sandstone riverbed changes to hard granite, and we reach the first of six cataracts. A *cataract* is a churning rush of water, where a river plunges through rocks and deep gorges.

- As we continue to follow the winding Nile, we go through two fertile areas — the first between the third and fourth cataracts, and the second south of the fifth cataract. Not far past the sixth cataract, the journey comes to an end at Khartoum, the capital city of present-day Sudan.

In ancient times, the climate of the Nile river valley was generally moister than it is now. Even then, however, the weather conditions were challenging: burning sun, high daytime temperatures, and harsh winds blowing across the Sahara Desert. But the people who lived in this area thousands of years ago learned to adapt to their natural environment, and take advantage of its many resources.

The first and most important resource was the Nile. During the June rainy season in the far-off mountains of Ethiopia the Blue Nile became swollen with water and muddy silt. This water and silt poured from the Blue Nile into the main Nile, causing it to overflow. After several months, the flood waters retreated and rich silt was left behind. Farmers planted seeds in this fertile soil.

The Nile provided fertile soil, water for irrigation, fish, and a way to travel. People used its mud to make pottery and bricks. The need to share this resource and learn how to use it skilfully were important reasons for people to co-operate, work together, and develop organized settlements. In this way, the Nile River became the source of life for ancient African civilizations. One of these was the Kingdom of Kush

The mud of the Nile was an important resource. Poorer people built their homes from sun-baked mud bricks. Wealthier people used bricks baked in kilns.

Nubia and the People of Kush

Find Lower and Upper Nubia on the map on page 113. Today, the region between the first and fifth cataracts of the Nile is still known as Nubia, although it does not exist as a separate country. This region is located mainly in northern Sudan, with a small section in southern Egypt.

These Sudanese workers are standing in front of the Royal Pyramids at Meroe. Beneath these pyramids, built more than 2500 years ago, kings and queens of Kush were buried. Nubian pyramids are generally smaller and steeper than those of Egypt.

In ancient times, different groups of Nubian people inhabited the entire area from Aswan all the way south to Khartoum. To the north of this area was Egypt, which is now recognized as one of the greatest of ancient civilizations. Egyptian customs and beliefs had a strong influence on the Nubians.

The early Egyptians were familiar with the skilled archers of Nubia, and called the region south of them *Ta-seti*, which means "land of the bow." Later, they began to refer to this region as Kush, a name that is also used in the Bible. Because of the dark skin of the Nubians, the Greeks and Romans called the region the "land of the burnt faces."

CHAPTER 1

Early settlements in Lower Nubia

The story of Kush begins thousands years ago.

Between 3500 and 2800 B.C., a group of people lived in Lower Nubia. At first they were mainly nomadic, but later they planted crops and used grinding stones for their grains. They also made superb pottery.

This handmade bowl is an example of the fine pottery made by the early settlers of Lower Nubia.

South of Nubia lay central Africa, a source of trade goods — ivory, ebony, animal skins, ostrich feathers, and gold. The people of Lower Nubia were in an ideal position to pass these goods on to Egypt, and they became active trading partners.

When Egypt became a united kingdom in 3100 B.C., its relationship to Lower Nubia changed. There were frequent raids in which prisoners were taken to be used as slaves. The now-powerful Egyptians travelled through Nubia and traded directly with regions further south. As a result, the first settlement in Lower Nubia came to an end.

c. 3500 B.C.
early settlement in
Lower Nubia

3100 B.C.
Egypt becomes
a united kingdom

c. 2800 B.C.
first settlement
comes to an end

This pattern between Egypt and Nubia repeated itself many times. When Egypt was strong, it dominated and exploited Nubia. When it was weak, Nubia thrived and grew wealthy from its control of trade routes.

About 500 years later, a second group of settlers in Lower Nubia appeared. Like the first group, the people hunted and farmed. Cattle were especially important to their economy, and were often illustrated on pottery and graves, and represented in small sculptures.

The Egyptians were generally weaker at this time, and they seem to have tried to maintain a good trading relationship. They got timber and cattle from Lower Nubia, and also travelled further south for goods like ebony, incense, oil, and leopard skins. During this peaceful period, for the first time Egyptian records mention a region known as the Land of Yam. Scholars believe that Yam was a Nubian settlement south of the third cataract, with its main centre at Kerma.

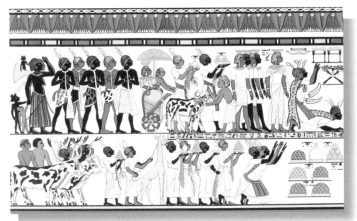

This copy of an ancient Egyptian tomb wall painting shows Nubian chiefs bringing presents to the Egyptian king.

Around the year 2000 B.C., Egypt regained its strength and conquered Lower Nubia. To secure their new territory, the Egyptians built massive fortresses along the Nile, which they maintained for more than 200 years. In part, they wanted to defend themselves against wandering groups of nomadic people who often attacked trade caravans. But they were also concerned about the strength of the Nubian settlement further south at Kerma, which they now referred to as Kush.

c. 2500 B.C.
Kerma settlement in
Upper Nubia

c. 2300 B.C.
second settlement
in Lower Nubia

c. 2000 B.C.
Egypt conquers
Lower Nubia

CHAPTER 2

Settlement at Kerma

Archaeologists believe that Kerma, just south of the third cataract, was first settled around 2500 B.C. Five hundred years later, Kerma was a well-established centre, with enough wealth and military power to worry the Egyptians.

The location of the Kerma settlement was important to its success. The area was ideal for growing crops and raising animals. Even more important was its position for trade. Goods from the south and east destined for Egypt came through Kerma, and since the people were strong and well-organized, they were able to control this trade.

These are the ruins of the Western Deffufa at Kerma, a huge structure that was probably the main religious building. Houses and workshops were located near this building.

In the middle of the 16ᵗʰ century B.C., Egypt decided to attack and destroy Kerma. The victorious ruler of Egypt returned home with the dead body of the leader of the Kush attached to the prow of his ship. The Egyptians went on to take control of Nubia as far south as the fourth cataract.

c. 1500 B.C.
Kerma destroyed
by Egypt

c. 1500 BC–1000 B.C.
Egypt controls
Nubia

c. 750 B.C.
King Kashta begins
the conquest of Egypt

Egypt controlled Nubia for about 500 years. But, as had happened so many times before, the time came when the Egyptians could no longer defend all their territory. They withdrew from the lands they had conquered, and Nubia was again free.

For several hundred years after this event, there are almost no records of what happened to the Nubians. But in the eighth century B.C., a new and powerful Kingdom of Kush appeared. Its first capital was Napata, but Meroe eventually became the main city of this kingdom.

Around 750 B.C., King Kashta of Kush began the conquest of Egypt. Before long, the Kush triumphed over Egypt, and its rulers were now the pharaohs of Egypt. They ruled both lands for about 80 years.

When Egypt regained control, the pharaoh had the names of the Kushite rulers of Egypt removed from many monuments. The Egyptians had always looked down on the Nubians, even going so far as to draw images of them on the soles of their sandals so that they could crush them as they walked. To have been conquered by these "vile" and "wretched" people, as the Egyptians described them, was an event to be erased from memory.

But the Kingdom of Kush continued to thrive for hundreds of years in Meroe. It slowly declined after the Roman conquest of Egypt. The Romans began to bypass Meroe as a trade route, and the city lost an important source of its income. Eventually, Kush was overrun by nomadic tribes from west of the Nile River.

655 B.C.
Nubians driven out
of Egypt by Assyria

23 B.C.
Queen Amanirens of
Kush fights Rome

320 A.D.
Malequerebar, last
king of Kush, is buried

IMAGING NUBIA

The ancient Greeks and Romans were fascinated by Nubia. Few of them had ever seen the land south of Egypt, but in their minds, it must have been a great civilization. After all, it was the source of marvellous goods — gold, ebony, ivory, incense, the skins of exotic animals, and giant feathers from ostriches. What a magnificent place it must be!

The Greek historian, Herodotus, provided one of the most imaginative description of the Nubians. About 430 B.C., after travelling as far south as the first cataract of the Nile, he reported that the Nubians were tall and handsome, and that their queen travelled in a palace on wheels that was drawn by 20 elephants. In his famous book, *The Histories*, he wrote that "most of them lived to be a hundred and twenty, and some even more...."

Until this century, the history and accomplishments of ancient Nubia and the Kingdom of Kush were almost unknown. Even today, after years of work by archaeologists from many countries, including Canada, only a small fraction of known sites have been excavated. In the future, there will be many new chapters in the story of Nubia and the Kingdom of Kush.

In July 2001, archaelogists from the Royal Ontario Museum announced the discovery of Dangeil, an ancient Nubian city long buried under the sands of Sudan. This exciting new discovery, shown here, will help the world learn more about the people of Nubia.

Life in the Kingdom of Kush

The Kingdom of Kush around 650 B.C.

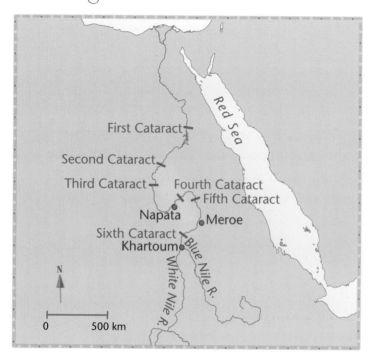

This map shows the Kingdom of Kush when its kings no longer ruled both Egypt and Kush. The kingdom extended north past the second cataract and south beyond Khartoum. The main centre was Meroe.

It is impossible to paint a detailed picture of life in Kush, especially of the lives of ordinary people. This is true of many civilizations, since ancient written records are usually about leaders and important events, not the day-to-day activities of farmers or other workers. Also, scholars trying to learn more about Kush face a unique challenge. By the second century B.C., the Kush had developed a writing system for their own language, Meroitic. The symbols they used are similar to those in Egyptian writing, and experts have managed to identify what sounds the symbols represent. But so little is known about the Meroitic language that the meaning of most inscriptions remains a mystery.

For these reasons, and also because archaeologists are still excavating and examining the evidence, a portrait of life of Kush remains incomplete. It is a work in progress.

This stele was found by archaeologists of the Royal Ontario Museum at the site of the city of Meroe. The meaning of the Meroitic inscription is still unknown.

IN THE IMAGE OF GOD: INTELLIGENT AND CREATIVE
RECORDING OUR LIVES

Understanding ancient writings is a great challenge. For a long time, no one knew how to read cuneiform, but the code was finally cracked about 150 years ago by Henry Rawlinson, a young English army officer who was also a student of languages. When Rawlinson was stationed in Persia, he saw a gigantic carving high up on the side of a cliff. It showed a mighty figure with his foot placed on the head of a defeated man while other conquered leaders stood nearby. Below this scene was over a thousand lines of cuneiform. No one knew what the writing said or who the powerful king was.

Taking his life in his hands, Rawlinson climbed up the cliff to copy all the markings so he could try to translate them. Eventually, he was able to figure out that the powerful king was Darius of Persia (521–485 B.C.), who had conquered his enemies and wished to show his greatness through this carving.

Part of the cuneiform writing on the carving says:
"Darius the King says: You who behold this inscription or these sculptures, do not destroy them, but protect them as long as you have the strength."

Written language is a powerful tool. It allows people to create a permanent record of their knowledge, ideas, feelings, experiences, and beliefs. After more than 2000 years, Darius, the King of Persia, can still speak to us.

Here is a story about another great ancient king who understood the power and value of written records.

Of all the civilizations that arose in Mesopotamia, the fierce Assyrians are among the most famous. One of the greatest Assyrian kings, Assurbanipal, loved literature, and he built an enormous library in his capital city, Nineveh, around 650 B.C. In this library, he gathered all the writings of the people he had conquered. He also sent his men to every city to collect more books for his library.

After his death, the Assyrian Empire was overthrown by the Babylonians, and Nineveh was burned. But instead of destroying the library, the fire preserved it. All the "books" Assurbanipal had collected were made not of paper, but of clay, and the fire had baked them hard. About 150 years ago, they were found and people today can once again read the first story ever written down — the adventures of the Mesopotamian hero, Gilgamesh.

This stone carving of Gilgamesh is more than 5 m tall. It was made in Assyria.

Economy of Kush

The area around Meroe received regular rain, and on this rich land people grew barley, millet, vegetables, dates, and cotton. Cattle breeding was important to the economy, both for trading and as a source of food. Further north, in Lower Nubia, the introduction of the waterwheel, which was driven by oxen, improved food production in these drier areas.

Since people, animals, and crops need a reliable source of water, reservoirs were dug around the area of Meroe to catch the water that fell during the rainy season. One of the largest of these reservoirs has a diameter of 250 m.

The city of Meroe was also the site of a large iron factory. The iron industry of Kush produced tools and weapons that were far stronger than those made of copper and bronze. The famous archers of Kush began to use iron-tipped arrows, and iron products became valuable items for trade.

Fertile land, abundant food, an iron industry, and highly skilled craft workers all contributed to the prosperity of Kush. But the main source of its wealth lay in trade. The area around Meroe was at the crossroads of several old and important routes. Trade caravans from central Africa passed through. Others travelled east to the Red Sea, or to settlements west of the Nile. Kush had valuable goods — cattle, iron tools and weapons, pottery, and gold jewellery. More importantly, it benefitted from being at the centre of trade.

This ancient stone statue of a lion holding a shield shows the power and confidence of the Kingdom of Kush.

Social and Political Organization

Most of the people of Kush produced food and provided labour for major construction projects — reservoirs, temples, pyramids, walls around settlements. These farmers and labourers were part of the lowest rank in the social structure.

Those with the highest rank included the ruler and royal family, the king's officials, and important religious leaders. The ruler had great authority. It is not clear whether the rulers of Kush were considered gods, but they were certainly seen as having a close relationship with them. If the harvest was poor, or the kingdom was threatened, the prayers of the ruler had special power. One of the greatest kings, Taharqo, was believed to have brought a long drought to an end because of his prayers for rain.

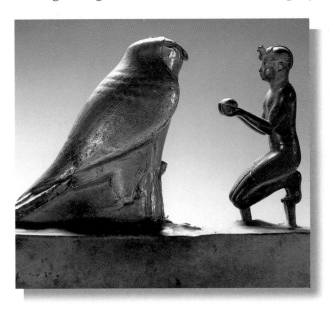

Taharqo ruled Egypt and Kush from 690–664 B.C. This sculpture shows Taharqo making an offering to the god Hemen.

In many kingdoms the ruler's oldest son usually inherits the throne. But in Kush, the inheritance passed through the women of the royal family. When a king died, the next ruler might be another offspring of the king's mother or one of the children of his sister.

The mothers and wives of rulers seem to have had an important role in Kush, and shared the duties of governing the kingdom with their sons or husbands. Inscriptions on their pyramids and monuments suggest that they were powerful figures in their own right. Beginning in the second century B.C., there were several female rulers of Kush.

Daily Life: Homes, Food, and Clothing

Most people lived in small homes made of sunbaked mud bricks. Some had just one room, while others had several rooms, with a courtyard on one side. The roofs were flat, supported by wooden beams. Wealthier Kushites used stone or fire-baked bricks for their houses.

In Meroe, archaeologists have identified the stone ruins of the royal palace where the ruling family lived, government offices, small temples, and a royal bath. This main city centre was surrounded by a stone wall.

Not everyone in Kush had a permanent home. Some people travelled from place to place with their herds, and needed a type of shelter that could be easily moved. These temporary homes were probably made from a mixture of mud, reeds, and animal skins.

Clay ovens, water pots, and flat pans for making bread have been found in the remains of homes. Most women probably had many daily tasks — baking bread and cheese, milking cows, weaving reed baskets, cooking meat and vegetables, and making bowls and pots for their family. The pots made by skilled artisans were intended for trade, not for daily use.

Making clothes was also likely a task for women. We know that leather was used, since leather garments and sandals have been found in burial sites. But we don't know if these were worn only by the wealthy, or if it was the custom to bury people in their finest clothes. Cotton and linen were also used for clothing.

Most likely, the children of farmers worked to help the family from a young age — collecting milk, planting and harvesting, and sharing tasks like cooking and making pots. Children of wealthy families may have received some education at the temple, and learned how to read and write.

Families probably looked forward to religious festivals and other celebrations connected to the farming year. They also relaxed by playing games in which dice and small round disks were used. These objects have been found in graves, as well as small pottery animals, which may have been toys.

Religious Beliefs

Life in the Nile valley was quite predictable. Each year, the floods came and watered the river valley. Each year, the flood waters retreated, and left behind rich soil for crops.

The sun and the river meant life, and the people of the Nile saw them as gods — the forces that created the world. Other gods were responsible for every aspect of life in this world — the places where people lived, the work they did, and natural events like childbirth and death.

The people of Kush worshipped many of the same gods as Egypt. Osiris, Isis, and Amun were especially important. But Kush also had its own gods. The most important of these was the lion-god Apedemak, who is associated with war and creation. He is always represented with a lion's head, and often with armour and weapons. Statues of lions were placed around temples and reservoirs for protection.

The Egyptians and Kushites believed in an afterlife, and in some kind of judgment following death. Those who had lived justly in this world would continue to exist in the next world. Those who were judged unworthy were devoured by a strange creature made up of parts of different animals — lion, hippopotamus, and crocodile.

The many items found in Kushite tombs — food, armour, weapons, jewellery, cosmetics, furniture — tell us that they believed their next life would be very much the same as their present one. In some royal tombs, the remains of a large number of people have also been found. These people were likely servants, guards, and female relatives of the ruler, and it is believed that they were probably buried alive.

This stone carving of Apedemak is on the wall of the Lion Temple at Naga.

Achievements of Kush

Many of the achievements of Kush are those associated with all great civilizations: a stable society that controlled a large amount of territory; an economic system that produced a food surplus; the construction of lasting monuments; the creation of a written language; a body of religious beliefs and practices.

Two further achievements are distinctively Kushite:

- Their pottery is among the very finest of any ancient civilization. The white clay that was used and the skill of the potters produced exquisite bowls, pitchers, and cups. Kushite pottery was traded, not just with Egypt, but throughout the Mediterranean.

- As far as it is known, the Kushites were the first African people to master the technology of working with iron. Because of their location at the crossroads of many important trade routes, it may be that they introduced this knowledge to other areas of Africa.

The location of Kush has given it a special place in history. For thousands of years it was the gateway to tropical Africa, whose precious metals and exotic goods were desired, first by the Egyptians, and later by the Greeks and Romans. Nubia lived in the imaginations of the ancient Mediterranean peoples as a place of fabulous wealth and mystery. Today, we continue to learn more and more about this vital and accomplished African civilization that flourished in the valley of the Nile.

This Kush jar, decorated with lion masks and other designs, was found in a tomb at Faras, in Sudan.

The Past in the Americas

NORTH AMERICA

SOUTH AMERICA

The Ancient Lands of Mesoamerica

Archaeologists use the word *Mesoamerica* for those parts of Mexico and Central America where civilizations developed long before Europeans arrived in this part of the world. *Meso* comes from a Greek word meaning *middle*, so the name *Mesoamerica* is a way of describing the land that lies between the continents of North and South America. The ancient region of Mesoamerica includes part of Mexico, the countries of Guatemala and Belize, and parts of El Salvador and Honduras.

Mexico and Central America in Modern Times

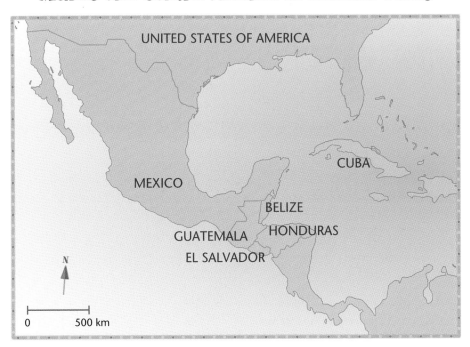

UNITED STATES OF AMERICA

CUBA

MEXICO

BELIZE

GUATEMALA HONDURAS

EL SALVADOR

N

0   500 km

In 1519 A.D., when the Spanish explorer Cortez and his men first arrived in Mexico, they were amazed by what they saw. The most important city of the Aztec Empire, Tenochtitlan, rose out of swampy land of the plateau of central Mexico, and had a population of over half a million people. There were magnificent stone temples and palaces, and floating gardens, called *chinampas*, on which produce was grown. Goods arrived at the great market of this city from all over the Empire — food, clothing, pottery, gold, silver, and jade.

But the Spanish invaders did not know that the Aztec Empire represented a late stage in the development of the people of Mesoamerica. Long before the Aztecs, there were the civilizations of the Olmec, of the unknown people who built the city of Teotihuacan, of the Maya, and of the Toltec. Of these ancient civilizations, scholars agree that the Maya was the greatest.

Maya Lands in Ancient Times

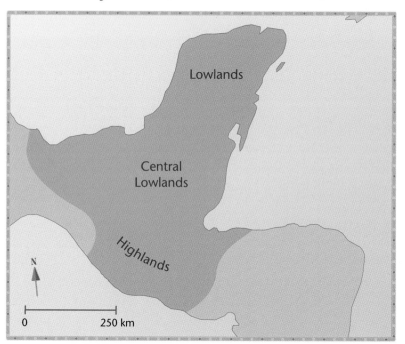

The map on page 130 shows the three main landform regions within the territory of the Maya:

- The largest landform region is the central lowland, much of which is covered with tropical rain forest. Daily temperatures are high and rain is frequent.

- The highlands are somewhat cooler, especially at night, and receive less rain. South of these highlands is a belt of active volcanic mountains that runs along the Pacific coast.

- The lowlands of the Yukatán peninsula are generally quite dry and flat, with thin soil and low scrub forest. The major water sources are underground caverns and channels.

The Maya lands lie within a tropical climate zone. Instead of the four seasons we experience, there are two seasons — dry from January to May, and rainy from May to December.

As it did in other places in the world, the change from being hunters and gatherers to being food producers took place over thousands of years.

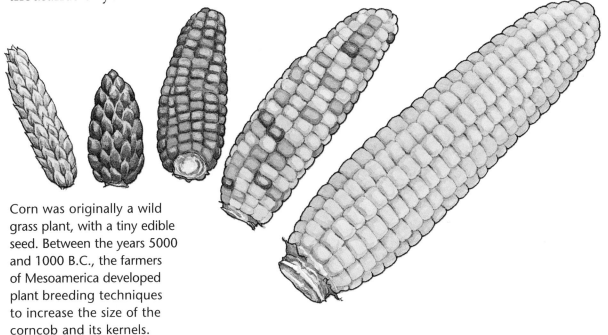

Corn was originally a wild grass plant, with a tiny edible seed. Between the years 5000 and 1000 B.C., the farmers of Mesoamerica developed plant breeding techniques to increase the size of the corncob and its kernels.

Corn, squash, and beans were the main diet of the early people of Mesoamerica. The first villages developed around 3000 B.C., and people soon began to make grinding stones and stone containers in which to store their seeds.

The earliest known civilization in Mesoamerica began about 1200 B.C. with the rise of the Olmec people, and lasted until about 400 B.C. The Olmec created large centres for religious ceremonies and made giant carved figures, using stone tools. They also developed technologies for making rubber, weaving cotton, and decorating pottery. The earliest calendar and hieroglyphic writing also began with the Olmec.

About 500 years after the decline of the Olmec, the largest city of Mesoamerica was built not far from present-day Mexico City. Little is known about the people who created and lived in Teotihuacan, which means "Places of the Gods," but their achievement is still a source of wonder.

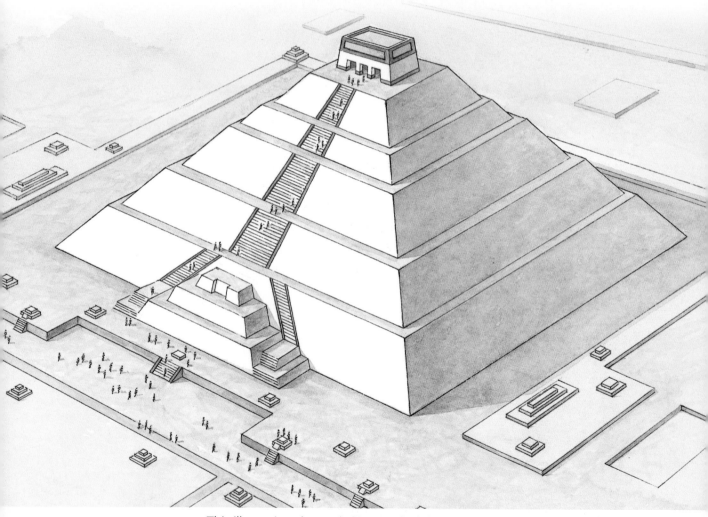

This illustration shows the Pyramid of the Sun in Teotihuacan. It is the largest and oldest building in the city. As many as 200 000 people lived in Teotihuacan. Around 750 A.D., a major fire destroyed large areas of the city.

The Maya

Like all ancient peoples, the story of the Maya begins with the establishment of farming villages. There is evidence of these small communities from about 1000 B.C.

The descendants of the ancient Maya continue to live in southern Mexico, Guatemala, Belize, and Honduras. Small homes in farming villages like this one are very similar to those built by the Maya thousands of years ago.

Men and boys were responsible for the main fields, and women and girls looked after the household — food preparation, cooking, and tending the gardens around the home. Crafts, such as weaving and making pottery and tools, were also part of village life. Handmade items like pots, decorated cloth, and tools were often exchanged for other goods and services.

Around 500 B.C., the Maya began to create cities and develop a more complex way of life. They built temples, pyramids, and palaces. Their knowledge of astronomy and mathematics expanded, as well as their use of calendars and a system of hieroglyphic writing. As this first chapter of Maya history came to an end, they had laid the foundation for a great civilization.

1200–900 B.C.
earliest Maya
farming villages

c. 600 B.C.
jade obtained
through trade

c. 500 B.C.
first cities
built

Maya cities multiplied and flourished, and become more or less independent kingdoms with their own rulers. By the third century, Maya kings were erecting steles and monuments with hieroglyphic inscriptions that recounted both their ancestry and the important dates and events of their reign.

The city of Palenque achieved its greatness during the seventh century A.D. under its ruler, Pacal. This photo shows the Temple of Inscriptions, which is also the burial place of Pacal. His tomb was discovered in 1949 by a Mexican archaeologist.

This was a time of remarkable achievements. The economy was strong, and valuable resources were traded throughout the region. There was great rivalry among the cities and competition led to frequent fighting.

Some archaeologists believe these conflicts contributed to the collapse of the Maya civilization in the southern and central regions. Climate changes and food shortages may also have played a role. Between 900 and 1000 A.D., city after city was abandoned, and buildings were left half-finished. The greatest period of Maya history had come to an end.

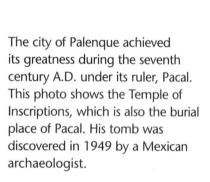

c. 450 B.C.
pok-a-tok first
played by Olmec

292 A.D.
first known
inscribed stele

c. 684 A.D.
Pacal, ruler of
Palenque, buried

After the great Maya cities of the southern and central regions were abandoned, many people moved to cities in the Yukatán peninsula. Uxmal, and then Chichén Itzá, became major centres of power. Finally, at the beginning of the 13th century, a new city called Mayapán was founded and remained in power for over 200 years.

At the top of this temple in Chichén Itzá, Maya priests observed the heavens through small windows. The placement of these windows was carefully planned so that the changing positions of the sun and the planet Venus could be seen and charted during the year.

Mayapán was sacked and burned by rivals in 1441, and no other city took its place as a major centre of power. When the Spanish arrived with their horses and guns, the Maya were soon overwhelmed.

The Spanish conquest was a brutal end to the Maya civilization. The people were forced to accept Spanish rule, and most became little better than slaves on land that had once been theirs. European diseases like small pox and measles, against which they had no immunity, killed many.

909 A.D.
last known lowland stele inscribed

C. 1200 A.D.
Mayapán founded

1524 A.D.
Spain conquers Maya lands in Guatemala

The earliest missionaries in Mesoamerica were the Franciscans, followed by the Dominicans. On many occasions, theirs were the only voices raised in defence of the native peoples. The Church played an important role in speaking out against injustice.

BARTOLOMÉ DE LAS CASAS

In 1515, a Spanish priest named Bartolomé de Las Casas began his work of defending the native people of Mesoamerica against exploitation by the Spanish. Through his efforts, new laws were passed forbidding the Spanish from keeping slaves. When he became Bishop of Chiapas, he continued his struggle for justice. He made it clear to the Spanish conquerors that if they refused to free their slaves, they were persecuting Jesus in his poor.

Sadly, some missionaries did not follow the Gospels. A Spanish priest named Diego de Landa severely punished the Maya who would not accept Christianity. He also burned a collection of their books that he believed were filled with the work of the devil.

Through a strange twist of fate, Landa became a major source of information about the very people he had mistreated. He had been a keen observer of their customs and farming methods, and was interested in their calendars and hieroglyphic writing. He wrote a report about the Maya and, about 300 years later, a copy of this report was found. It was eagerly read by scholars trying to understand the lost civilization of the Maya.

1561 A.D.
Landa burns
Maya books

1592 A.D.
Spain forbids
forced labour

1863
Landa's report
discovered

Life in the Great Cities of the Maya

They give an entirely new aspect to the great continent on which we live, and bring up with more force than ever the great question: Who were the builders of these American cities?

John Stephens wrote these words about the ruins that he and Frederick Catherwood explored between 1839 and 1842. Their descriptions of once great and now abandoned cities captured the imagination of many people. Before long, archaeological expeditions began and knowledge about the Maya grew. But the most important source of information — their hieroglyphic written records — remained a mystery for some time.

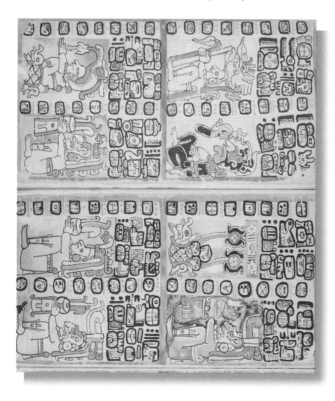

These are pages from one of four surviving Maya books. Researchers believe that the Maya created hundreds of books, known as *codices*, which were written on paper made from bark. A single book is called a *codex*. These pages come from the Madrid codex, named for the city in which it was found in the 19th century. The few remaining codices were helpful in solving the mystery of Mayan hieroglyphs.

By the middle of the 20th century, scholars finally began to make progress cracking this code. Today, about 80% of hieroglyphic symbols can be deciphered. This achievement, as well as many ongoing archaeological investigations, has led to a much better understanding of the history, religion, and political and social organization of the Maya.

Economy of the Maya

Goods and services were collected and redistributed in cities and towns through a system of tribute. Tribute is something like our present-day taxes:

- Lesser kings and nobles paid tribute to powerful kings in the form of natural resources and manufactured goods. They might have also supplied workers or soldiers.

- Farmers paid tribute with food and services.

- After a battle between two kingdoms, the loser paid tribute to the winner.

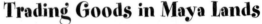

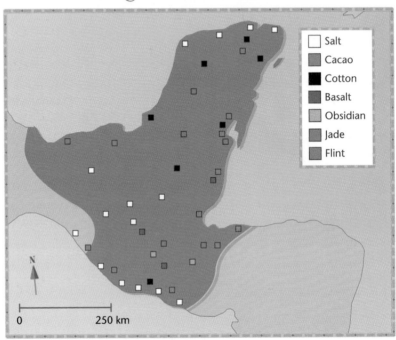

Markets and fairs were held at various times during the year. Some of these were connected to religious festivals. Fairs were also opportunities for merchants to arrange exchanges of goods.

Goods were not purchased with money, but were exchanged using a barter system. Cacao beans, however, were so valued that they came to be used as if they were money. A drink made of ground cacao beans and pepper was considered a mark of high social rank, and was enjoyed by the wealthy.

As archaeologists began to discover just how many people lived in and around the great cities, they became curious about Maya farming practices. How did the Maya manage to produce enough food?

With the common slash-and-burn method, trees and bushes are cut down at the start of the dry season, left to dry, and then burned just before the rainy season begins. Planting, weeding, and harvesting follow. After a few years, however, weeds become difficult to control and the soil is exhausted. Fields must be left to rest for as long as seven to ten years, and new ones prepared.

This method was used by the Maya without the help of metal tools, ploughs, or sturdy farm animals. There were no native animals suitable for pulling vehicles, and because of the swampy land of the rain forests, wheels were not practical. Trees were cut down with stone axes, and soil was dug with a pointed stick.

But it is now known that this was not the only way in which the Maya produced food. They also:

- planted fruit and breadnut trees in small gardens around their homes. The nuts from the breadnut tree are highly nutritious.

- built stone walls in hilly areas to prevent erosion. These walls held back the soil, and created terraces that were used for planting.

- created raised fields surrounded by a network of canals in swampy areas. This type of land use can support intensive agriculture. Many experts believe that the canals were used not just to manoeuvre around the fields, but also to raise fish.

Breadnuts

Since most large Maya cities were near rivers, swamps, or lakes, it seems likely that the technique of using raised fields was what made it possible to feed a large population.

IN THE IMAGE OF GOD: INTELLIGENT AND CREATIVE
FINDING SOLUTIONS

Human beings are problem solvers. It is part of our nature to invent new ways of doing things and to use our knowledge to improve our lives. Just as the Maya found a way to produce more food, so other people around the world have come up with ingenious and useful ideas. Here are two examples.

You might not realize it, but if you go for a bike ride today, take the bus home, or check the time on your classroom clock, you are relying on one of the greatest technological inventions of all time — the wheel.

This world-changing invention was thought up by some unknown person over 5000 years ago in Mesopotamia. From then on, people were no longer limited to the strength of their own legs, arms, and backs.

No one is sure exactly how wheel making began. Perhaps the very first wheel was made of solid wood cut from a tree trunk. Soon wheels began to be made from smaller wood planks held together by cross pieces. These wheels were very heavy and soon pieces of the wood were cut out to make the wheel lighter. Eventually, spokes, just like those on a bike, were used.

Among the earliest uses for this new technology were the potter's wheel, wagons for transportation, and, of course, chariots for war.

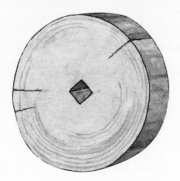 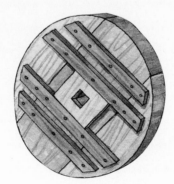 

The story is told that one day the great Greek scientist Archimedes overheard a man complaining that he had injured his back lifting something. While listening, Archimedes noticed two children standing on opposite ends of a plank of wood balanced on a stone. A third child came along and joined her friend at one end of the plank. The balance was broken. The three friends got off the plank and moved it so that one end was nearer the stone. When they got back on, the plank balanced again.

Archimedes instantly realized the importance of what he had seen. He rushed home and placed one end of a long piece of wood under a boat, put a log under the wood close to the boat, and, with one hand, lifted it! His experiment worked. He set to work to explain how one of our most important tools worked — the lever. Here is the law of the lever:

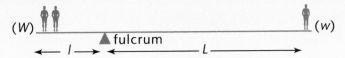

The weight of an object (W) on one side of the support (fulcrum) will balance the weight of an object on the other side (w) of the fulcrum if the length of the plank of wood from the fulcrum to the first object (l) multiplied by W is equal to the length of the plank of wood from the fulcrum to the second object (L) multiplied by w. In other words, both sides will be in balance when the weight of the heavier object multiplied by the shorter length equals the weight of the lighter object multiplied by the longer length. Here is the formula: $W \times l = w \times L$

After he had worked out the formula, Archimedes said, "Give me a place to stand and a long enough lever and I will move the world." What did Archimedes mean?

Social and Political Organization

At the top of the social and political hierarchy of the Maya were:

- the rulers of the great city kingdoms and their families. A king had several roles — lawmaker, military leader, and priest. Most rulers were considered to be descended from the gods. The inscriptions on their steles and monuments proclaim their ancestry and their great deeds, and the massive pyramids in which they were buried are a visible symbol of their high rank.

Ah Cacau, who ruled the city of Tikal from 695 to 723 A.D., is buried beneath this pyramid. At the top of the structure is a sculpture of him sitting on a throne and looking out over the main plaza of his great city.

- important nobles who carried out the king's wishes. Some of them may have been in charge of small settlements that were part of a larger kingdom. Others served as merchants who arranged trade agreements. The chief priests of city kingdoms were also part of this social rank.

There were several groups in the middle ranks of the social hierarchy:

- The highest ranking nobles most likely passed on the king's orders to less important officials — people who could organize labourers and artisans for a construction project and make arrangements to locate and transport the necessary materials.

- Another group was made up of people who had special knowledge and skills — the surveyors or architects, who created plans for monumental building projects; priests, who led religious ceremonies and maintained the calendars; scribes, who were trained by the priests to read and write hieroglyphic symbols.

- Expert masons, carvers, plasterers, and painters were required for the construction of monumental buildings. There were other skilled artisans who created decorated pottery and stone tools, or carved jade.

Those with the least status and power were labourers, farmers, and slaves:

- Each large building project required many labourers to quarry the stone, haul it to the building site, and put it in place. Farmers were needed to produce food, but also likely sometimes served as labourers.

- Slaves occupied the lowest rank of the social hierarchy. This group included people captured during a conflict and some who lost their freedom as punishment for a crime.

What is not known about Maya society is whether there was movement within the ranks. Could a labourer learn the skills of masonry or carving and move up in social rank? Could a talented minor official eventually become an important adviser to the king? These are questions that cannot be answered yet.

Daily Life: Homes, Food, and Clothing

Wealthy people lived in stone houses that had several rooms, sometimes built around a private patio. Farming families lived near their fields. They built small houses on top of a mound of earth or stones so that rain water would drain from the dirt floor. The roof was thatched with palm leaves or grass, and the walls were made with wooden poles tied together with vines. A household often included parents, children, and grandparents or other relatives.

Women were responsible for the household. Porridge and *tortillas* (flatbreads) made from cornflour were cooked each day over a small stone hearth. A farming family's regular diet included corn, beans, yams, peppers, and wild fruits like bananas and papayas. On special occasions, deer or wild pig was served.

Because of the warm climate, not a lot of clothing was needed. Soft cotton was the finest fabric, but a coarser cloth was made from yucca plants. Men wore loincloths, and women wore loose, embroidered dresses or skirts with long blouses.

The ancient Maya constructed their hearths with three stones, set in the shape of a triangle. This shape was considered sacred, since they believed that the gods had constructed a cosmic hearth of three stars on which the world was centred. A three-stone hearth is still used today in many Maya homes.

Jade beads, which were greatly valued, and other decorations made from shells and feathers were very popular, especially among wealthy people. Tattoos and body paint were also used by both men and women. The dress of wealthy nobles was quite ornate — long capes made from jaguar skins, and headdresses with feathers from a sacred bird called the quetzal. Unlike peasants, who usually went barefoot, nobles wore sandals made from deer hide or jaguar skin.

Every culture has ideas about physical appearance, and what characteristics are especially desirable. For the ancient Maya, these included pointed front teeth, crossed eyes, a flattened forehead, and a large nose. During the first months of life when the bones of the skull were still flexible, babies wore a wooden frame to flatten their foreheads, and a bead was dangled just in front of their eyes to make them cross-eyed. Some people filed their front teeth, and filled in the spaces with pieces of jade.

Boys and girls from farming families worked with their parents from the time they were five or six. Young girls wore a red shell on a string around their necks until they were about 12 years old. After that, they were considered ready for marriage. Newly married couples lived with the wife's family for several years, and the husband worked with his father-in-law. After he had proved himself, they moved into their own home near his parents.

Religious Beliefs

The world of the Maya was filled with gods who influenced every aspect of life. If there was a drought, it meant the rain gods were displeased. If the harvest was plentiful, then the corn god was content.

The Maya depended on the gods to make the sun shine, the rain fall, and the corn grow. But they also believed that the gods depended on them for worship and nourishment. The great Maya temples, their religious ceremonies and festivals, and the sacrifices they offered were expressions of this belief about the relationship between gods and humans.

One of the ways the Maya communicated with their gods was by offering their blood. Since they believed they could nourish the gods, on important occasions people cut themselves using a spine from a stingray and let the blood drip onto a piece of bark that was then burned. This ritual had the greatest power when it was performed by the king, since he was so closely connected to the gods.

The Maya also communicated with the gods by sacrifices — gifts of food or an animal. On occasion, there was human sacrifice, usually of prisoners of war. In the period when Maya civilization was in decline, this practice became more frequent.

This photograph shows a small statue of a smiling harvest god.

Maya priests played an important role, not just in religious rituals, but in every aspect of life. Because of their special knowledge, it was believed that they could predict the outcome of future events — a new baby's fortune in life, the richness of a harvest, or the right time to go to war. They based their predictions on a complex series of calendars that they developed and maintained.

MAYA CALENDARS

A method of recording time is important in all societies, especially those that depend on farming. But the Maya were intensely interested in time for another reason. They believed that days and numbers were associated with gods who controlled the fate of humans. By understanding which gods were powerful at which time, they could better control their destiny.

The Mayas had three calendars:

- **a sacred calendar** with 260 days, divided into 20 day names and 13 numbers. This calendar was used to plan religious ceremonies.

- **a solar calendar** with 365 days, divided into 18 months of 20 days each, and a final short month of 5 days, which was considered a very unlucky period. An extra day was added every four years, just as we do in our leap year.

- **a long count calendar** with the year 3114 B.C. as its starting point, perhaps because of the belief that this was the date of the last creation of the world.

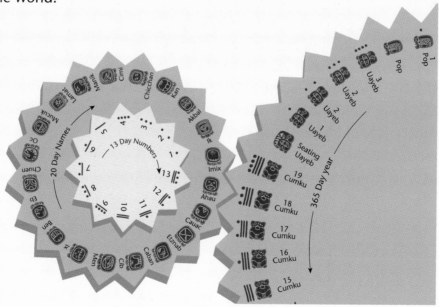

Each day had a day name and number from the sacred calendar and a month name and number from the solar calendar. As this illustration shows, the date is 13 Ahau, 18 Cumku. Because the two calendars had different lengths, it took 52 years before a date would be repeated. The beginning of a new 52-year cycle was an occasion for a great festival.

MAYA MATHEMATICS

The great interest of the Maya in recording time led them to develop a complex number system that used just three symbols. Unlike our number system, which is based on a unit of 10, the Maya based theirs on a unit of 20.

Here are the Maya numbers from 0 to 19. A shell is 0, a dot is 1, and a bar is 5.

0	1	2	3	4	5	6	7	8	9

10	11	12	13	14	15	16	17	18	19

When we reach the number 10, we move one column to the left. When the Maya reached 20, they moved one row up. A single dot in the second row up now represents 20. Here are the numbers from 20 to 25.

20	21	22	23	24	25
• (1 X 20)	• (1 X 20)	• (1 X 20)	• (1 X 20)	• (1 X 20)	• (1 X 20)
(0 X 1)	• (1 X 1)	•• (2 X 1)	••• (3 X 1)	•••• (4 X 1)	—— (5 X 1)

In our number system, we move another column to the left when we reach 100 (10 x 10). The Maya moved up to a third row when they reached 400 (20 x 20). Each single dot in the third row up now represents 400. Here are the numbers 465 and 823.

465
• (1 X 400)
••• (3 X 20)
—— (5 X 1)

823
•• (2 X 400)
• (1 X 20)
••• (3 X 1)

Can you figure out these Maya numbers?

Achievements of the Maya

When John Stephens and Frederick Catherwood first saw the great Maya cities, they knew they were in the presence of a remarkable people. But, in fact, the greatest Maya accomplishments are not their temples, palaces, or monuments. Other Mesoamericans created impressive city centres, and also developed farming techniques to support a large population. These are important, but are not the reason the Maya are considered the greatest early civilization in the Americas.

The greatness of the Maya lies in the capacity of their minds. Their advanced understanding of astronomy and mathematics and their complex system of writing set them apart, and are splendid achievements.

Astronomy — Without the use of telescopes or other sighting instruments, Maya priests were keen observers and recorders of the cycles of the sun, moon, and planet Venus. The Dresden codex, one of the few remaining Maya books, contains records of their observations over 104 years. Experts have determined that their figures are amazingly accurate. For example, their calculation of the long and complex cycle of Venus is in error by only 14 seconds per year.

For the Maya, knowledge of astronomy served a religious purpose. Since the planet Venus was considered a war god, it was important to calculate its cycle accurately. Along with the sacred calendar, this information was probably used to plan battles or determine if sacrifices were needed.

Mathematics — As far as we know, the mathematical idea of zero and a symbol to represent it originated in only two places in the world — India and Mesoamerica. It may seem like a simple idea, but it is a remarkable intellectual achievement.

In India, Hindu mathematicians created a numbering system with a zero around 600 B.C. Arab traders came to know this system, and through them, it eventually spread to Europe during the Middle Ages. We use this system today.

Not long after, on the other side of the world, the Maya also grasped the concept of zero, and went on to invent a unique number system using only three symbols.

Written language — The complex system of Maya hieroglyphic writing, the only fully developed written language that originated in the Americas, is an astonishing achievement.

Scholars have made great progress in decoding the symbols or *glyphs*, as they are called, but there is still much to be learned. They know that the glyphs are a mixture of *ideographs*, signs that stand for ideas, and syllables representing sounds. Often two glyphs are combined to express a single idea, or there is a main sign with smaller signs that provide additional information.

This is the glyph for Pacal, ruler of the city of Palenque from 615-684 A.D. The shield on the left side is an ideograph glyph. The Maya word for shield was *pacal*. The three small glyphs on the right side are the syllables *pa*, *ca*, and *la*. Put together they sound out the ruler's name, Pacal.

There is much that we do not know, and will never know, about the Maya. Think of the missing books that would provide information about their history and way of life. The continued work of archaeologists and other scholars will help us grow in our understanding. But like John Stephens, we will always want to know more about the gifted and mysterious people who created a great civilization in the rain forests and highlands of Mesoamerica.

The Past in Asia

ASIA

The Middle Kingdom

From earliest days, the people of China have called their land the "Middle Kingdom" because they believed it was the centre of the world. Everything outside was unimportant. This map shows the Huang He River flowing from deep in the heart of China. Like the Nile in Africa, it floods frequently and leaves behind a fertile silt. Along the Huang He, also known as the Yellow River because of its yellow-coloured silt, farming communities developed around 3000 B.C. These settlements were the beginning of Chinese civilization, the longest-lasting in the world.

China in Modern Times

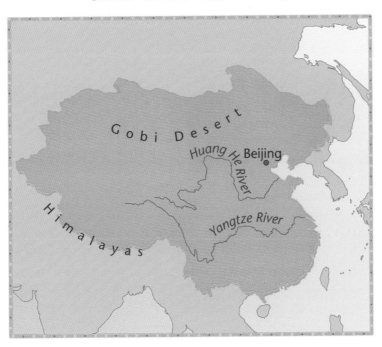

Gobi Desert

Huang He River   Beijing

Himalayas

Yangtze River

The many farming communities in the Yellow River valley gradually grew into small states led by chieftains. The most powerful chief eventually became king and when kingship was passed on from father to son, the ruling family became known as a *dynasty*.

Over time, people moved southwards to the Yangtze River valley, where the climate was warmer and wetter. Hundreds of small states developed, and two early powerful dynasties — the Shang and then the Zhou — were established. However, the peaceful times of these dynasties ended, and for almost 500 years the many states of China fought each other for power. This time is known as the "Warring States Period." Finally, by around 250 B.C., the state of Qin defeated all the remaining states. For the first time, all China was united under one rule. The king of Qin took the name Shi Huangdi — First Emperor.

During the Shang dynasty, writing and silk weaving first appeared, and the Chinese became skilled at casting in bronze. Under the Zhou kings, the chest-strap harness for horses was invented, something not seen in Europe for another 2000 years.

When the 2500-year-old tomb containing these bronze bells was opened in 1978, they were still hanging in their proper place. The middle row is for playing the melody and the bottom row is for the accompaniment.

c. 3000 B.C.
farming communities
on the Yellow River

c. 1600 B.C.
Shang dynasty
established

c. 1550 B.C.
first silk
weaving

Shi Huangdi was a cruel ruler. He kept a large army and centralized all authority. He replaced the conquered ruling families with military governors who ran the new provinces under his control.

Shi Huangdi unified his empire by draining swamps, clearing land, and building roads, bridges, and canals. To keep out barbarians from the north he joined together all the military fortifications and built the Great Wall. To make trading and tax collecting easier, he standardized weights, measures, and money across the empire.

The Great Wall of China is Shi Huangdi's greatest building achievement. It is the world's longest human-made construction, and is the only one that can be seen from space.

One of Shi Huangdi's most controversial reforms was his decree that writing should also be standardized. Writers and teachers resisted because it meant that much of the knowledge and writings of the past would be unreadable. In response, Shi Huangdi ordered all books to be burned except those dealing with medicine or farming. Scholars who resisted were killed.

When this extremely unpopular emperor died, rebellion broke out. The victorious rebels were led by a peasant named Liu Bang, who established one of the most famous and important dynasties in Chinese history — the Han Dynasty.

c. 1500 B.C.
writing developed

551–479 B.C.
Confucius

c. 500 B.C.
Lao Tzu

Liu Bang, who took the name Gao Zu (Forefather), was a very different man than the first emperor. He was an uneducated peasant, simple in manner, and with a forgiving nature. But he was also a fierce and determined fighter, and a shrewd and intelligent leader. Gao Zu followed the saying of the Chinese philosopher Xunzi: "The prince is the boat. The common people are the water. The water can support the boat, or the water can capsize the boat."

He kept many of the reforms and the centralized government established by the first emperor, but replaced harsh laws with simpler ones. He restored order after the long civil wars, freed prisoners, gave land to his followers, reduced punishments, and encouraged learning.

Although he ruled for only seven years, Gao Zu made an enormous impact. The dynasty he founded ruled China for four centuries, a golden time of growth, power, and great achievements.

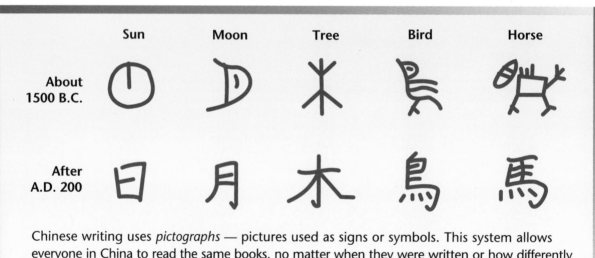

	Sun	Moon	Tree	Bird	Horse
About 1500 B.C.					
After A.D. 200					

Chinese writing uses *pictographs* — pictures used as signs or symbols. This system allows everyone in China to read the same books, no matter when they were written or how differently people say the words. The language of mathematics is similar — the meaning of the symbol "5" doesn't change whether you say "five" (English), "cinq" (French), or "funf" (German).

480–221 B.C.
Warring States
period

221 B.C.
Shi Huangdi,
First Emperor

210 B.C.
completion of Shi
Huangdi's tomb

Perhaps the greatest Han emperor was Wu Di, who ruled for 54 years (141–86 B.C.). He extended the borders of the empire as far south as Viet Nam, as far north as Korea and Manchuria, and deep into the west. He used diplomacy and trade when he could and fought when he had to. To keep good relations with the northern barbarian tribes, he sometimes sent noble women to marry their chiefs. One of these women, Princess Xi-Chun, wrote a poem to express her grief.

> *My family married me off*
> *to the king of Wusan*
> *a million miles from nowhere.*
> *My house is a tent.*
> *My walls are of felt,*

> *Raw flesh is all I eat,*
> *with horse milk to drink.*
> *I always think of home*
> *and my heart stings.*
> *O to be a yellow snow-goose*
> *floating home again!*

China During the Han Dynasty

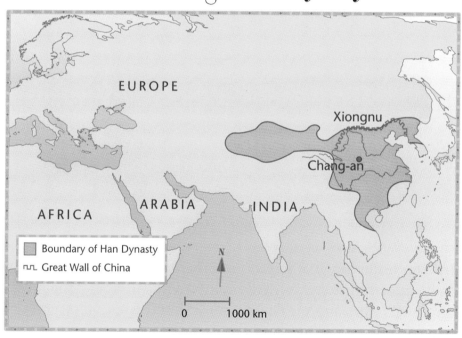

206 B.C.	**141–87 B.C.**	**125 B.C.**
Han dynasty	Emperor	Silk Road
begins	Wu Di	established

Since Wu Di wanted the most talented men in his government, he made a dramatic change. Instead of relying on friends or noble families, he issued the following proclamation:

Heroes Wanted!

Exceptional work demands exceptional men. A bolting or a kicking horse may eventually become a valuable animal. A man who is the object of the world's detestation may live to accomplish great things. As with the intractable horse, so with the infatuated man —
it is simply a question of training.
We therefore command the various district officials to search for men of brilliant and exceptional talents,
to be OUR generals,
OUR ministers,
and OUR envoys to distant states.

The candidates were given a written test and the emperor himself made the final selections. From that time on, working for the government was highly valued and considered the most important work anyone could do. By 1 A.D., the civil service had 130 000 people.

124 B.C.
Imperial University
established

c. 100 B.C.
invention of
the wheelbarrow

31 A.D.
Chinese learn to
how to make steel

As part of his goal of expanding the empire, Wu Di sent one of his generals, Zhang Qian, to find a nomadic tribe called the Yuezhi. Wu Di hoped to create a military alliance with them since they were also the enemies of the Xiongnu, the fierce northern barbarian tribe who had fought with the Chinese for hundreds of years.

Ten years later, General Zhang returned to say that he had found the Yuezhi, but they did not want to fight the Xiongnu. Wu Di's disappointment was soon replaced by excitement about the stories he heard. General Zhang had travelled as far west as present-day Afghanistan and had seen remarkable people and places. Wu Di was amazed to learn that Chinese goods, especially silk, were highly valued in these unknown lands. The emperor decided to develop a trade route to these places. The route was long and dangerous, so he made treaties with the tribes along the way to allow trade caravans to pass safely.

The Silk Road

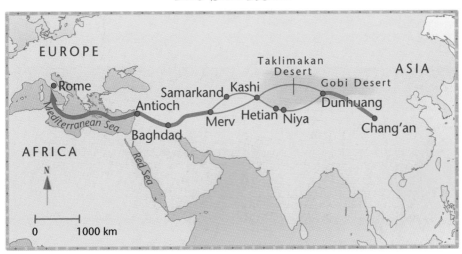

The 6400 km long trade route known as the Silk Road carried Chinese goods west to India, Afghanistan, the Middle East, and even as far as Rome. Romans knew China as Serica, the "Land of Silk." European desire for Chinese silks and spices was an important reason for later explorers sailing to North America. They were looking for a shorter and easier route to China.

c. 65 A.D.
first Buddhist
missionaries visit China

c.100 A.D.
Sima Qian writes *Shih Chi*,
the first history of China

c. 105 A.D.
invention
of paper

The Han dynasty ended the way many empires seem to end. The emperors were weak leaders, the nobles became corrupt, the peasants became unhappy, and the barbarians saw a good opportunity to invade. A writer from that time described what he saw:

> Nowadays people are extravagant in clothing, excessive in food and drink, and fascinated with clever language. They become expert in the arts of deception. Some men never learn how to handle ploughs and hoes .... many women do not cultivate cooking.... The rich compete to do better than one another while the poor are ashamed that they cannot keep up.

In addition, natural disasters, like floods, added to the social breakdown. When the last Han emperor fell in 220 A.D., 400 years of fighting and struggle followed. Stability finally returned to China with the Tang Dynasty (618–907 A.D.).

During the Han dynasty, daily life was recorded on stones made for the tombs of the wealthy. This rubbing from a stone shows two military riders. Because of constant raids by northern barbarian tribes, the Han emperors kept a large cavalry.

132 A.D.
Zhang Hen invents
the seismograph

166 A.D.
first recorded contact between
China and Roman Empire

220 A.D.
Han Dynasty
ends

Life in the Han Dynasty

The Economy of Han China

Farming was the backbone of the Han economy. Around the Yellow River, grains like wheat, barley, and millet were grown. To make as much use of the fertile yellow silt as possible, long narrow fields were arranged in terraces. In the warmer south, near the Yangtze River, rice was produced.

Two thousand years after the Han dynasty, terraced farm fields are still used by farmers in China.

Villages were responsible for local water use, but the government constantly worked on large-scale water improvements by building canals, wells, and drainage systems. It was important to have a water supply during times of drought and to control flooding as much as possible.

Although a farmer's life was very hard, there were many inventions to make work easier. The wheelbarrow, known as the "wooden ox," was invented about 100 A.D., more than 1000 years before it appeared in Europe. Sometimes a sail was fitted to a wheelbarrow to use wind power. A seed drill allowed farmers to plant their crops in rows, making sowing, weeding, and irrigation more efficient. Iron ploughs were also produced in large iron foundries.

Crops besides rice and grains included hemp for clothing, bamboo for construction and writing materials, and fruits such as peaches, plums, and melons. The most valuable extra crop, however, was mulberry trees.

SILK

For at least 3500 years the Chinese have made some of the world's most beautiful silk. By the time of the Han, silk was China's most important trading good. For centuries, the technology of silk making was kept secret. Anyone who revealed it was punished by death. Here is their secret.

A farmer would grow as many mulberry trees as he could and his wife would cultivate silkworms, which are caterpillars of a kind of moth. She kept them on special shelves away from rain and sun, and every day would feed them their favourite food — mulberry leaves. The sound of the caterpillars eating was said to be like rain beating down on a tin roof. The caterpillars would spin a cocoon made of one long, fine, but strong thread.

This photograph shows a detail of a beautiful silk cloth preserved from the Han period.

The cocoon would be dipped in boiling water to separate the thread, which would then be wound onto reels. One thread might be a kilometre long! The thread was then wound together into strands and dyed different colours. Then the silk would be woven into cloth on a loom.

Chinese silk was also used as a surface on which to write and even paint.

Coal was discovered early in the Han dynasty and metals and minerals, including iron ore and salt, were mined. The iron and salt industries were so important that the government took control of them. By 31 A.D., a water-powered furnace produced temperatures so hot that iron could be turned into steel, which was called "great iron."

Factories, run by civil servants, produced bronze and other metalware, crafts, iron weapons and tools, and many other goods.

Social and Political Organization

Like almost every early civilization, the social and political structure of the Han dynasty was hierarchical. At the head of society was the emperor and his family.

- **The emperor** — Early in Chinese history the idea had developed that the emperor was a "Son of Heaven" who had been given his position by the highest spiritual authority in the universe. His right to rule was called the *Mandate of Heaven*. A harmonious and well-governed society meant that the emperor held the Mandate of Heaven. But if society were troubled by unhappy people or serious natural disasters, this was a sign that the Mandate of Heaven was lost and perhaps a new dynasty was about to take over. One important way the emperor kept harmony was by fulfilling his religious duties of prayers and regular rituals.

- **Civil servants** — Over the years, government officials gradually replaced the nobility in importance. A centralized and large state needed good officials, and Emperor Wu Di's advertisement for the best people marked the beginning of a new system known as *meritocracy*, or "rule by the best." The civil service exam was very difficult, and people prepared for many years. Candidates had to know from memory all the books of Confucius, China's greatest teacher and thinker. Poetry was so highly prized that writing beautiful poetry was also an important part of the exam.

  Meritocracy allowed people to cross social ranks. Gongsun Hong, a former swineherd, rose to become chancellor of China, one of the highest positions in the government.

- **Farmers** — Emperor Wu Di once said, "Farming is the foundation of the world." China, with its very large population, needed lots of food, and farmers had high social status. But their lives were often harsh. Their heavy taxes supplied most of the money to run the empire, and they also owed military service and labour for public works projects.

Here is a very old farming song that describes their hard life. Some farmers sang, while others hit the ground to keep time as they worked.

> *When the sun comes up we work,*
> *when the sun goes down we rest.*
> *We dig a well to drink,*
> *plough the fields to eat —*
> *the Emperor and his might — what are they to us!*

- **Artisans and Skilled Workers** — Although not regarded as highly as farmers, these people received social respect because of the valuable work they did.

This beautiful bronze sculpture was created by a Han artist.

- **Merchants** — Even though they often became very wealthy, merchants ranked very low socially. Because they sought only to make money and did not grow food or make useful things, they were seen as looking out for their own good and not for the good of society.

- **Servants, Entertainers, Slaves** — Servants and entertainers held the lowest social status, except for slaves. There were few slaves in Han China, and they had rights that slaves in some other civilizations did not. For example, it was against the law to kill a slave, and two princes were disinherited for ordering slaves to be executed.

Daily Life: Homes, Food, and Clothing

Poor farmers lived in simple one-room thatched huts made from *wattle and daub* (wood with mud plaster). Homes of wealthy people were often made with brick walls and tiled roofs, and had two and sometimes more courtyards. Many had beautiful ponds and gardens, which were considered important places for spiritual nourishment.

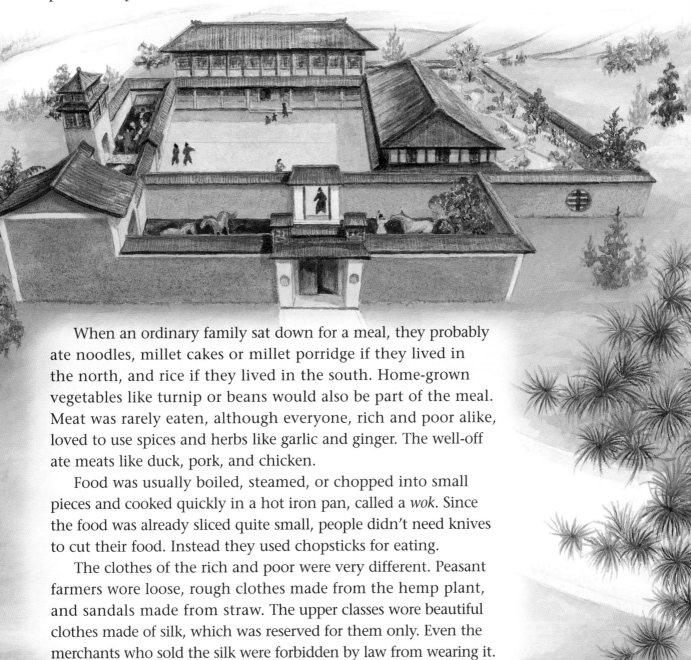

When an ordinary family sat down for a meal, they probably ate noodles, millet cakes or millet porridge if they lived in the north, and rice if they lived in the south. Home-grown vegetables like turnip or beans would also be part of the meal. Meat was rarely eaten, although everyone, rich and poor alike, loved to use spices and herbs like garlic and ginger. The well-off ate meats like duck, pork, and chicken.

Food was usually boiled, steamed, or chopped into small pieces and cooked quickly in a hot iron pan, called a *wok*. Since the food was already sliced quite small, people didn't need knives to cut their food. Instead they used chopsticks for eating.

The clothes of the rich and poor were very different. Peasant farmers wore loose, rough clothes made from the hemp plant, and sandals made from straw. The upper classes wore beautiful clothes made of silk, which was reserved for them only. Even the merchants who sold the silk were forbidden by law from wearing it.

The most important festival of the year was the New Year Festival. Family members gathered to share food and exchange gifts. The dragon, a symbol of wisdom, strength, and good luck, was a sign of the New Year. This festival is still celebrated today.

Games of chance were very popular and people enjoyed playing card and dice games. Playing cards were invented by the Chinese and so were kites. Originally kites were used to frighten the enemy in battle, but later they were used in celebrations.

Even today, China is famous for its amazing kites.

Sometimes performances would be held in the local marketplace and people would flock to see jugglers, acrobats, fire-eaters, magicians, storytellers, and more.

Music was an important part of life. Confucius himself was so moved by some music he heard that he said "he forgot the taste of meat" for three months. Music was played at religious ceremonies, and rich households employed musicians who played drums, gongs, pipes, bronze bells, and stringed instruments like the qin, which made a gentle, sad sound.

Religious Beliefs

Unlike the Nile, the flooding of the Yellow River was unpredictable. Sometimes there would be fearsome floods that destroyed farmlands; sometimes there would be terrible droughts. At times, the flooding was so severe it even caused the river to change its course completely. Because of the misery this caused, the Yellow River became known as "China's Sorrow."

This uncertainty helped form the early Chinese belief that the forces of nature needed to be kept in balance. If the harmony of the world was disturbed, disasters could easily result. It was important for humans to understand nature's balance and make adjustments to keep the world in harmony.

The two underlying forces of the world to be kept in balance are known as *Yin* and *Yang*. Yin is Earth, the dark, the moon, the feminine; Yang is Heaven, the light, the sun, the masculine. These two forces are not opposed to each other. Both are necessary but must work together.

Another feature of Chinese religion is *ancestor worship*. People believed that the spirits of those who had died watched over living family members. Every home had a shrine for honouring ancestors.

There are three great teachings that have had an enormous influence on life in China — Daoism, Confucianism, and Buddhism.

This ancient symbol shows the balanced relationship of yin and yang.

- **Daoism** — The earliest teachings of Daoism are found in a short book called *Tao te Ching*, written by Lao Tzu, a teacher who lived during the long years of war before the Han dynasty. Daoists believe that people should not be ambitious for wealth, power, or status, which lead only to war, ruin, and death. Instead, they should live simple lives in harmony with nature by following the *Tao* or "the Way," the underlying principle of life.

- **Confucianism** — The most influential person in the long history of China is Confucius, a wandering teacher who lived during the Warring States Period. Most rulers during this time adopted a code called *legalism*, which offered a very simple approach to governing: Be very harsh and force people to do what you want. Emperor Shi Huangdi was a Legalist. Confucius strongly opposed Legalism, and with his disciples he travelled from state to state teaching how society should be organized and how people should live.

Confucius

Confucius saw the family as the model for society. In a harmonious family, the structure was hierarchical and every member had well-defined duties, obligations, and status. Husbands ranked higher than wives, parents ranked higher than children, older children ranked higher than younger ones. But all family members should show proper respect and kindness to the others as they fulfilled their roles.

Society should be organized in a similar way. In a harmonious state, rulers had the interests and welfare of their people at heart and in return the people gave them obedience and loyalty.

Confucius knew this system could only work if citizens and rulers were morally good. His views on right and wrong were a central part of his thought. Here are some of his teachings from a book called *Analects*, put together by his disciples after he died.

- *"A worthy man understands what is right. An inferior man understands what is profitable."*

- *Tzu Kung asked: "Is there one word that can serve as a principle for the conduct of life?" Confucius said: "Perhaps the word 'reciprocity.' Do not do to others what you would not want others to do to you."*

Most rulers did not listen to Confucius during his lifetime, but from the Han dynasty until almost our own day, he has been honoured in China as the greatest teacher who ever lived.

- **Buddhism** — Wu Di's Silk Road was not only a way for goods to travel between China and the outside world. It was also the way that the religion of Buddhism travelled from India to China during the Han dynasty.

  Buddha, which means "Enlightened One," is the name given to an Indian prince called Siddhartha. Siddhartha had lived a comfortable life in his father's palace, with no real experience of suffering. One day when he left the palace, he saw that the lives of ordinary people were filled with hardship, pain, and death. He was shocked by what he saw and gave up his princely life to find out how to end suffering.

  After many years, he understood that people's desires were the cause of suffering. If we could end our attachment to things, our suffering would end. This moment of realization was when Siddhartha became the Buddha. He began to teach his ideas of simplicity and non-attachment and Buddhism soon spread throughout India and into China.

IN THE IMAGE OF GOD: INTELLIGENT AND CREATIVE
LEARNING TO LIVE TOGETHER

Thinkers in every civilization try to figure out the best way to govern. Confucius taught that harmonious relations and balance made for good government. More than 1000 years earlier, people in Mesopotamia came up with the new idea that laws applying to everyone were an important part of good government.

When Hammurabi became king of Babylon in 1750 B.C., he was surrounded by dangerous neighbours. Slowly, over 30 years, Hammurabi defeated them one by one until he was the ruler of an empire.

To give his empire stability and security, Hammurabi established a Law Code that would apply to everyone. He had the laws inscribed on steles and put up in major cities. The Code was intended "to make justice appear in the land, to destroy the evil and the wicked that the strong might not oppress the weak...." Here are some of Hammurabi's laws:

- "If a doctor has operated and saved a man's life he shall be paid 10 shekels. If the patient dies, the doctor's hand shall be cut off."

- "If a noble destroys the eye of another noble, his own eye shall be destroyed."

- "If a son has struck his father, his hands shall be cut off."

- "A builder who sells a poorly constructed house that collapses and kills its owner may be put to death."

This stele of Hammurabi's Law Code was found 100 years ago. The 282 laws are written in cuneiform.

Over 2500 years ago, the people of Athens, the greatest city-state in ancient Greece, began a new experiment in government. They rearranged the social hierarchy and came up with a new system, which they called *democracy* ("rule by the people"). Under this system, every citizen of Athens could speak and vote on important state matters. This kind of democracy is called *direct democracy*.

Athenian democracy is the ancestor of the system we have today in Canada, but there are some important differences. Our system is called *representative democracy* because we choose leaders to represent us and make decisions on our behalf. Citizenship in Athens was also much more controlled than it is in Canada. Women, foreign residents, those under 18, and slaves could not be citizens and had no say in running the state.

Aristotle

The Greeks also gave us *philosophy*, the study of the way things really are. One of the greatest philosophers was Aristotle, who wrote these words about democracy: "In a group of people, each member is an ordinary person. It you regard them not as individuals, however, but as a group, they may very likely be better than a small number of exceptional people. A feast to which many contribute is better than a dinner provided by a single person." (*Politics* Book 3:11)

Achievements of the Han Dynasty

You have already learned about some of the discoveries and inventions of the Han. Here are just a few other valuable scientific achievements from that time.

Paper — The first paper was made from silk rags, but soon hemp, bamboo, and mulberry bark were used. First, the raw material had to be soaked for a long time to soften it. Then it was boiled and pounded into a pulp. A fine screen was dipped into the pulp to collect a thin film of mushy pulp fibres. Pressure was put on the screen to remove extra water and then the screen was left to dry. Finally, the finished sheet of paper was peeled off the screen.

Surprisingly, at first paper was not used for writing but for clothing or hygiene. A text from 93 B.C. tells of a palace guard advising a prince to cover his nose with a piece of paper — perhaps to cover a sneeze. Soon, however, there was a great demand for writing paper and the government started to mass-produce it.

Compass — The magnetic compass was first used to make sure that houses were built facing in the direction most in harmony with energy forces of nature. Later it was used to help ships navigate the seas.

Seismograph — Zhang Heng, a Han civil servant, invented the *seismograph*, a device used for detecting earthquakes. An earthquake tremor caused a device inside the bronze machine to release a ball from a dragon's mouth where it would be caught by one of the toads. From this, people would know the direction of the earthquake vibrations. It could detect an earthquake almost 500 km away.

Zhang Heng's seismograph

Medicine — The Chinese believed that illness was caused by an imbalance in a person's yin and yang. Doctors recommended a balanced diet and also used herbal medicines to restore health. Hundreds of herbs were used. *Xu duan* (teasel root) was used to help broken bones heal. *Guo qi zi* (wolfberry) was used to improve eyesight. *Sheng ma* (bugbane rhizome) was used for headaches and colds.

Chinese doctors also used *acupuncture*: very thin needles were inserted into different points on the body to relieve pain and restore the body's harmony. Today, the practice of acupuncture has spread all over the world.

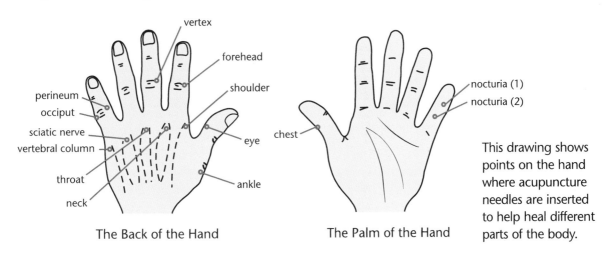

The Back of the Hand

The Palm of the Hand

This drawing shows points on the hand where acupuncture needles are inserted to help heal different parts of the body.

The Han period was also a time of great artistic achievements.

Literature — Poetry had always been valued in China, but the standardization of writing, a long period of peace and prosperity, and the growth of education led to a great outpouring of literature during the Han dynasty.

In 25 B.C., the Han emperor ordered copies of all literary works to be brought to the capital. He wanted his own library to be complete and also to make sure that he had correct versions of everything. The list that was prepared still exists, and we know that his library had ancient sacred writings, books on philosophy, mathematics, astronomy, farming, medicine, war, history, grammar, geography, and, of course, poetry.

The *Shih Chi*, "Records of the Historian," written by Sima Qian in 100 A.D., was one of the earliest and greatest history books. In more than 130 chapters, Sima Qian recorded all of Chinese history up to his own time. He was the first to base his writing on facts and not on myths and guesses.

Writing has been an important part of Chinese civilization from its earliest days. This photograph shows some of the earliest Chinese writing carved on bone.

Bronze — Beautiful and complicated work in bronze was created very early in Chinese history. This bronze figure shows a horse with one hoof delicately balanced on a bird. This "flying horse" is a reminder of the magnificent horses that had come to China along the Silk Road.

Horse sculptures were popular in Han China.

Lacquer — Lacquer work was valued by the Han upper classes because of its light weight and beautiful colours. Artisans would apply many thin coats of lacquer — sometimes up to 200 — over a base of carved wood or bamboo. Lacquer is hard and strong when it dries, and it was even used on military equipment like shields. Mineral powders added to the lacquer created vivid colours. Artists would paint delicate flowers or designs on the lacquer object.

This lacquered dish was found in the tomb of a noble from the Han dynasty. The hardness of the lacquer preserved it perfectly for more than 2000 years.

Han society welcomed human intelligence and creativity, and nourished these gifts by emphasizing the importance of education and learning. This solid social foundation helped later Chinese dynasties to flourish. Even today, in far-off Canada, our lives are better for the contribution the Han made to the human family so long ago.

The Past in Europe

A Settlement on the Tiber River

Rome's story is a remarkable one, but not simply because of the size of the territory it controlled. The story has a special significance for people of the western world because the heritage of this great civilization is still alive today in Europe and America. It is alive in languages, in systems of government and laws, in art and architecture, and in intellectual life.

And it all started in a small farming settlement on the Tiber River.

Italy around 750 B.C.

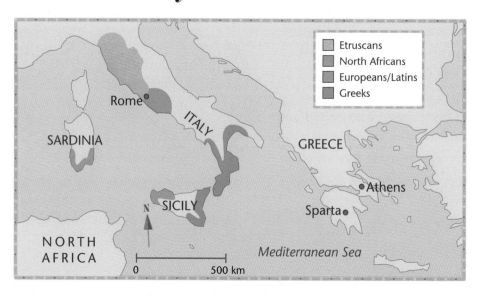

Beginning around the year 1000 B.C., there were small farming villages on the seven hills that overlooked the Tiber River, near the site of present-day Rome. The land was fertile and easy to defend. The Tiber served as an important means of transportation, and two trade roads met not far from the farming villages. The people of this area grew grain and herded animals, and lived in small circular wooden huts with straw roofs.

A great empire needs noble origins, and the following legend of the founding of Rome was cherished by its people and celebrated by Roman historians.

Long, long ago, twin boys named Romulus and Remus were born. Their mother was the daughter of King Numitor of Alba Longa, a city in Italy, and, according to the legend, their father was Mars, the god of war.

King Numitor was overthrown by his brother, who ordered that the infant boys be drowned in the Tiber River. They were rescued by a female wolf, who cared for them as if they were little cubs. Later, a shepherd found the boys, and raised them.

When Romulus and Remus became men, they restored King Numitor to the throne. An oracle told them to build a great city on the banks of the Tiber, with Romulus as its king. On April 21st in the year 753 B.C., Romulus marked out the boundaries of Rome with his plough.

Remus was jealous of his brother, and jumped over the new boundary. Because of this disrespect, Romulus killed him. After a long reign as the first king of Rome, Romulus magically disappeared in a thunderstorm

c. 1000 B.C.
small farming villages
on the Tiber

753 B.C.
founding of
Rome

509 B.C.
Rome's last king
expelled

According to tradition, seven kings ruled Rome, although most historians believe there were probably more. These rulers were chosen by the *patricians*, who were the powerful and wealthy heads of old Roman families. Patricians also served as members of the *Senate*, which was the body that advised the kings.

One of the last kings of Rome, Servius Tullius (578–535 B.C.), made a number of important changes in the way the city was governed:

- Roman citizenship was granted to all who settled in the city.

- A census was held, and all citizens were classified according to their wealth: land, goods, livestock, and grain. For the first time, land was not the only measure of wealth. The census recognized the importance of skilled artisans, traders, and merchants to the economy of Rome.

- The army was reorganized. All male citizens, not just the patricians and their servants, were expected to participate. The army was divided into *centuries*, which were units based on wealth. Those with the most money were in the cavalry, since they could afford horses and expensive armour. Those who could not afford even slingshots or bows and arrows provided support services.

The final king of Rome, known as Tarquin the Proud, was expelled from the city by the Senate in 509 B.C. because of his harsh rule. The Romans developed a new and revolutionary form of government. They were determined that there would be no more kings who abused their power. Instead, the people would choose their leaders. The era of the Republic of Rome had begun.

451 B.C.
Rome's first
written laws

312 B.C.
first aqueduct

c. 310 B.C.
first Roman
road built

IN THE IMAGE OF GOD: INTELLIGENT AND CREATIVE
EXPLAINING OUR STORY

Legends like the one about Rome's founding are not "true" in the sense that the events actually happened. But they are true in a deeper sense. People all over the world have always used myths and legends to explain their origins, honour heroes and gods, and celebrate achievements. Such stories are a way of saying: This is who we are. This is what matters to us. This is the way we understand the world.

Mount Olympus, the highest mountain in Greece, was believed to be the home of a large family of gods. Just like any family, the Olympians were sometimes kind and generous, and sometimes selfish and mean. The Greeks loved stories about their gods.

The most important was Zeus, the king of the gods. When he was angry, he threw lightning bolts and roared with thunder. Hera, his wife, was the goddess of marriage and childbirth. Other important gods included Apollo, Aphrodite, Ares, Demeter, and Hermes. Athena, a favourite with the Greeks, was the goddess of wisdom and the arts.

Every four years, a sports competition was held to honour Zeus. All Greek cities, even those at war, participated in this event, known as the Olympic Games. The first Olympic Games were held in 776 B.C.

Like the Nile River in Egypt and the Yellow River in China, the Ganges is the most important river in India. The source of this river lies high in the Himalayan Mountains, believed to be the home of the gods, where the goddess Ganga lived.

One day Ganga was commanded to leave her home in heaven to provide life-giving water to humans on earth. She came to earth in the form of a river, flowing first over the sky, where she can be seen as the Milky Way. In one version of the story, Ganga was so unhappy at having to leave her home that she planned to flood the earth and destroy everything in her path.

But the god Shiva spread out his thick hair to capture all the water descending from heaven before it could destroy the earth. Then Shiva slowly released the trapped water by squeezing it from his hair.

From that day to this, the Ganges has flowed gracefully down from the Himalayas to the plains. The river's sacred waters attract millions of Hindu pilgrims, and temples can be found all along its 1500 km length. Every 12 years, as many as 12 million people come to the Kumbha Mela festival at Allahabad to purify themselves by bathing in "Mother Ganga."

The word *republic* comes from two Latin words — *res publica* — meaning "a matter for the people." But how were the people to participate? Would the concerns of all groups in Roman society be addressed?

The most important government members of the Republic were:

- **Consuls** — Two men from the patrician class were elected as consuls for a one-year term, and were in charge of both the army and government. Although powerful, they could take action only if both agreed.

- **Senate** — The Senate was made up of patricians who served as advisers to the consuls. They were not elected, but their influence was great.

- **Assemblies** — There were two assemblies, drawn from all citizens of Rome.

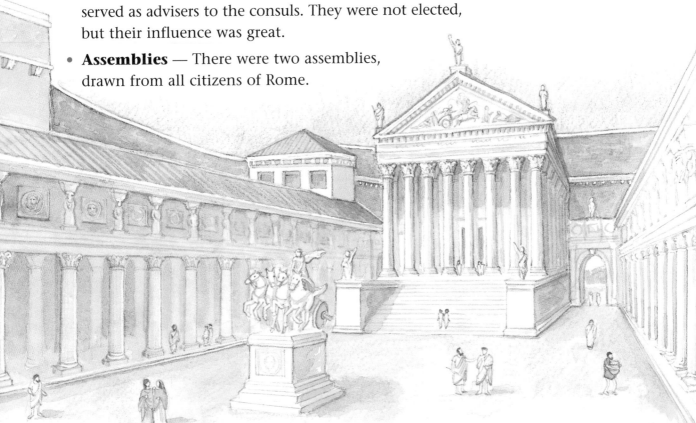

The Roman Forum, at the heart of the city, was the centre of government.

264 B.C.
first known record
of a gladiator contest

218–201 B.C.
Hannibal fights Rome
in second Punic War

133 B.C.
Tiberius Gracchus
presents land-reform law

Soon, however, a large group of Roman citizens called the *plebeians* grew dissatisfied. Most Romans were plebeians — ordinary working people. Many were farmers, but there were also artisans, storekeepers, and traders.

The story of the Republic of Rome is in part the story of the struggle of the plebeians to have more say in the government and to have the same rights as patricians. It took time, but they did have some success:

- In 494 B.C., plebeians achieved the right to elect their own representatives, called *tribunes*. Tribunes were chosen each year, and had the power to veto decisions of the consuls.

- In 445 B.C., plebeians were given the right to marry patricians.

- By 336 B.C., a plebeian could be elected Consul of Rome.

- Finally, in 287 B.C., the assembly of the plebeians won the right to pass laws without the consent of the Senate.

These reforms were important, but the government was still dominated by the patricians. Since elected officials were not paid, few plebeians could afford to participate in political life. Also, the right to vote did not include women and slaves.

The story of the Republic of Rome is also the story of great conquests. Through a series of wars and alliances, the Romans took control of all of Italy. They then turned their eyes to the rest of the Mediterranean world. Among their greatest rivals was Carthage in North Africa.

It was inevitable that Rome and Carthage would go to war, a conflict that lasted for more than 100 years. There were three wars in all, and both sides lost thousands of soldiers. But Rome was ultimately victorious in each war. For Carthage, the end of this long conflict was a bitter one. In 146 B.C., the Romans burned the city to the ground. All of its people, about 50 000, were made slaves.

73 B.C.
Spartacus leads
slave revolt

65–8 B.C.
the poet
Horace

58–51 B.C.
Julius Caesar
conquers Gaul

OVER THE ALPS WITH HANNIBAL

Of the three wars between Rome and Carthage, called the Punic Wars, the second is the best known because of Hannibal, the brilliant Carthaginian military leader. In the end, he was defeated; but for almost 15 years, he and his army fought with great skill and courage.

The years between the first and second Punic wars had been more like a truce than a final end. Carthage had never accepted its defeat, and began to acquire more territory in what is now Spain and southern France. In 218 B.C., Hannibal attacked the city of Saguntum, which had a treaty with Rome. Rome sent an army, but by the time it arrived, Hannibal and his troops were gone. Rome also sent a second army to Africa, but he was not there either.

Hannibal's March

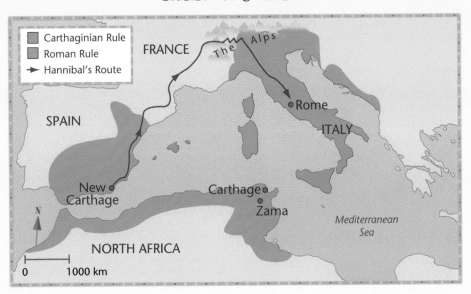

Instead, Hannibal had led his army of about 40 000 men and 40 war elephants north, over the Alps, and then south into Italy. Only 12 elephants and about 26 000 men survived this treacherous journey. But despite these losses, Hannibal's strategy worked. He surprised the Romans, and won several major battles. The war finally came to an end when the Romans attacked Carthage. Hannibal hurried home to defend the city, and in 202 B.C. he was defeated at Zama. The second Punic war was over.

Although Rome controlled most of the territory around the Mediterranean by 100 B.C., the Republic was in trouble. Divisions within society were growing deeper, especially between the rich and the poor. Small farmers were being crowded out by wealthy landowners. Since there were many slaves available for farming, citizens without land had few options. Many moved to the city of Rome, where there was high unemployment.

Reform was needed, and a tribune named Tiberius Graccus proposed that large estates be broken up and land be given to the poor. Members of the Senate, many of whom were wealthy landowners, disagreed, and Graccus was murdered.

Julius Caesar is famous for his military skill. He conquered the fierce Celts in northern Gaul (now northern France), and also crossed the English Channel and defeated several Celtic tribes in Britain. His book — *The Gallic Wars* — is still read today.

The noble idea of the Republic deteriorated into constant clashes and conspiracies. For a time, it seemed as if Julius Caesar would be able to restore order. But in 44 B.C., when he declared himself "dictator for life," he was stabbed to death.

Caesar's adopted son, Octavian, was more cautious. He eventually took control of Rome, and in 27 B.C. the Senate gave him the special titles of *Augustus* and *princeps*, which mean "revered one" and "first citizen."

Octavian kept the old traditions, but elected officials no longer had the power to rule. This power belonged to Augustus, as he was now known. The Republic of Rome had come to an end.

30 B.C.
Rome conquers
Egypt

14 A.D.
Emperor Augustus
dies

c. 30 A.D.
Jesus is
crucified

Augustus was a wise ruler who brought order to the Empire. He established a large civil service to look after the day-to-day business of government, and beautified Rome with many new buildings and temples. After years of unrest, the Romans were at peace.

During the 500 years of the Roman Empire, there were 66 emperors. Unfortunately, not all were as capable as Augustus. In fact, there are a few who are remembered mainly for their disgraceful actions:

- Caligula, emperor from 37– 41 A.D., insisted on being addressed as a god. Because of his extravagance, before long there was no money left in the treasury. He ordered a tax on the sale of food and demanded that the rich leave their money to the Empire. If they disagreed, he had them executed and took their property. The guards assigned to protect Caligula put an end to his disastrous rule by assassinating him.

- Nero became emperor in 54 A.D. at the age of 16. He is best known for having had his mother assassinated, and he may have set the terrible fire that swept through Rome in 64 A.D. Because Nero insisted that members of the nobility attend public performances in which he sang and played the lyre, the Roman author Suetonius reported that some members of the audience "feigned death and were carried out as if for burial" to escape. Nero's neglect of the Empire led to uprisings, and rebellion in the army. He was sentenced to death by the Senate, but took his own life.

Caligula made some very strange decisions, which led some people to think he was insane. For example, he made his horse a consul and had a marble stall built for the animal.

43–46 B.C.
Britain is
conquered

70 A.D.
Emperor Titus
destroys Jerusalem

72 A.D.
construction of the
Colosseum begins

But Rome was also blessed with a number of outstanding leaders who served the Empire and its people wisely. The task of governing was difficult, even for the most talented leaders. Among the challenges were:

- the high cost of running and defending a vast Empire
- the number of poor people in the city of Rome
- the desire of the provinces to have more say in the Empire
- controlling the army
- maintaining a good relationship with the Senate

The best of the emperors worked tirelessly to meet these challenges. During the years between 96 and 180 A.D., a series of gifted people led the Empire to its greatest glory. Here are just two of them:

Hadrian's Wall was 120 k long and had 17 forts. He built it to keep out the fierce Picts and Scots. Today, people enjoy visiting its remains.

- Hadrian (117–138 A.D.) was an accomplished military leader from Spain. He is especially well known in Britain because of the wall that he had built to mark the northern boundary of the Empire. Hadrian made a special effort to encourage talented people from the provinces to serve in government. He also ensured that Roman laws were applied in the same way throughout the Empire.

- Marcus Aurelius (161–180 A.D.) is well known as a scholar and writer. In the first part of his reign there was peace and a sense of unity in the Empire. But in the last years he was faced with many disruptions caused by barbarian tribes.

79 A.D.
Mount Vesuvius erupts and destroys Pompeii

122–128 A.D.
construction of Hadrian's Wall

212 A.D.
all free men in the Empire are made Roman citizens

The Roman Empire at its Height

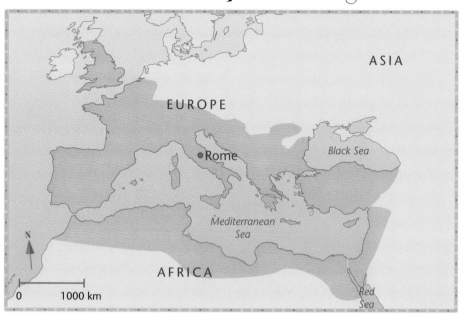

After Marcus Aurelius, Rome was again weakened by civil wars and power struggles. Diocletian, emperor in 284 A.D., did manage to restore order, but at a great price. He strengthened the army, raised taxes to very high levels, and divided the Empire into two parts — the Eastern and Western Empires.

When Constantine became emperor in 312 A.D., he too brought in higher taxes and increased the power of the army. But these measures could not restore the Empire. Its western part was under constant attack by barbarians, and the people suffered from unbearably high taxes. When Constantine built a new capital city in the Eastern Empire, his action marked the beginning of the end for the Western Empire.

Barbarian tribes pushed into Italy and sacked the city of Rome in 410 A.D. Then, in 476 A.D., the last Western emperor was deposed by a barbarian chief. This was the final event in the story of the great Roman Empire.

313 A.D.
Emperor Constantine
becomes a Christian

476 A.D.
last Western
Emperor deposed

519–534 A.D.
Justinian's Code
of Law

Life in the Roman Empire

There are farmers from the Balkans here, natives from southern Russia bred on horses' blood, people who drink the Nile's water and even those from far away Britain. Arabs, people from the shores of the Red Sea, as well as those from southern Turkey, have hurried here, and German tribesmen and Ethiopians each with their own peculiar hairstyles.

The Roman poet, Martial, wrote these words in 80 A.D. He was describing the people who came from all over the Empire for the opening of the Colosseum.

The Colosseum, Rome's greatest amphitheatre, is one of the most famous buildings from the days of the Roman Empire. It held up to 50 000 people. They sat in tiers of seats that circled the arena, which was the large open space in the centre.

Historians estimate that the population of the Empire at its height was between 50 and 80 million. If you could ask a few of these people about their lives, you would hear many different answers. The life of a blacksmith's family from Britain would be very different from that of a farming family in the Nile valley. A slave in Gaul would know nothing but labour, while a successful poet from the city of Rome might describe leisurely dinners and his beautiful villa.

Yet despite such differences, these people had something very important in common: They were part of an empire that, at its best, tried to achieve its ideals of honour, peace, prosperity, and justice.

The Economy of Rome

Agriculture was at the heart of the economy of the Empire. Vast quantities of wheat and barley were shipped from Egypt and North Africa to feed the one million people living in the city of Rome.

The provinces of the Empire were a source of great wealth. They provided many essential goods, such as foods, metals for tools and weapons, horses, wool, and paper. They also provided slaves, who were bought and sold throughout the Empire. Luxury goods from countries outside the Empire, such as silk from China and spices from India, were especially popular.

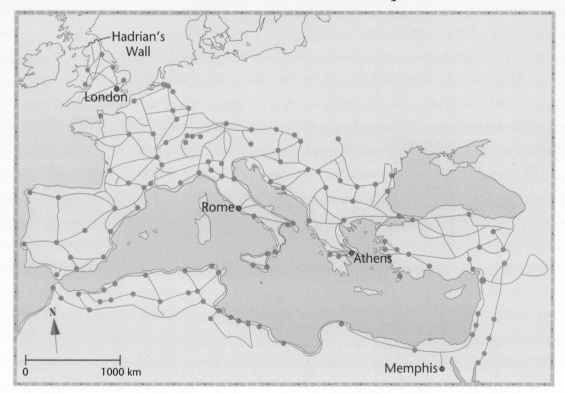

Roman roads were essential for trade. Their main purpose, however, was to provide a reliable route for the army and government officials. In all, 80 000 km of sturdy roads linked every part of the Empire. This map shows how Roman roads connected all the Empire's population centres.

The Roman economy also depended on a complex system of taxation. Tax inspectors visited every part of the Empire to assess the value of homes, businesses, and farms. Like today, taxes were also paid on goods that were bought and sold.

In the first two centuries of the Empire, the economy was strong and the tax system was well run and generally fair. In return for their taxes, people received important services like roads, running water, a well-organized army that provided secure borders, and a court system that administered justice fairly.

This aqueduct in France was probably constructed in the second century A.D. Roman aqueducts look like bridges, but at the top there is a channel that carries the water. They were built with a slight downward slope so that the water would run downhill. Once it reached the city, it was collected in large storage tanks. From there, pipes carried it to fountains and to public baths and toilets.

But as the cost of defending the Empire increased, taxes rose to unbearable levels. Most of the money was used for the army, rather than for other public services. Also, the army needed so many men that farms were neglected and food prices rose. This decline in the economy contributed to the collapse of the Empire.

Social and Political Organization

The people of the Roman Empire were part of a social and political hierarchy in which their ranks were based mainly on the amount of influence and power they had. But there was another important feature determining status: citizenship. Citizenship had a special significance for the Romans, and a number of distinctions were made that affected people's rights and status:

- The most important distinction was between a citizen and a non-citizen. A Roman citizen had rights and duties that were laid out in the law. A non-citizen was subject to the law, but did not have the right to vote or engage in trade.

- The rights of citizenship did not include women, children, and slaves. Only free men could be citizens.

- In some of the provinces, people were granted only partial citizenship. For example, they might have the right to trade and to marry a citizen, but not the right to vote.

THE RIGHTS OF A ROMAN CITIZEN

When St. Paul was arrested for stirring up demonstrations in Jerusalem and was about to be flogged, he asked a simple question: "Is it legal for you to flog a Roman citizen who is uncondemned?" Paul had been born a citizen in the Roman province of Cilicia. His question not only prevented the flogging; it also made the soldiers who had arrested him quite afraid. They had violated the rights of a citizen of Rome, an offence for which they could be punished. This story about St. Paul is found in the Acts of the Apostles (21–27).

At the top of the hierarchy was the emperor. Although there were still consuls and a Senate, consuls were no longer elected and did not have the power to pass laws. They were chosen by the emperor, who was the sole law-maker.

This system had strengths and weaknesses. In the hands of wise and dedicated men, the Empire was well run, the army was kept under control, and the government served the people. In the hands of less capable men, there were many problems.

Below the emperor were several groups with both high social status and political influence:

- **Senators, governors of provinces, army commanders** — In most cases, men from wealthy families filled these roles, but it was possible for a talented person to rise to this rank.

- **Wealthy businessmen** — It was considered beneath the dignity of noble Roman families to engage in business. Activities like trading, banking, and money-lending were carried out by members of the business class of society, many of whom became quite prosperous. Although their social status was lower than that of the nobles, their wealth allowed them to live in luxury, and to influence government decisions.

The Praetorian Guard, a unit of 900 men who guarded the Emperor, became increasingly important. In times of crisis, the Praetorian Guard had enough power to determine who would be the next emperor.

- **Writers** — Writing was valued by educated people, and some authors achieved high social status. Ancient Rome produced a number of great writers, such as Cicero, Catullus, Virgil, Horace, Livy, and Ovid. Many of these authors came from wealthy families and had the financial freedom to pursue their writing. But there were some important exceptions. Plautus, who wrote popular comedies, was a plebeian who worked in a bakery until he achieved success with his plays. Horace, a famous poet, worked as a clerk until the nobleman who employed him decided to support him so that he could spend all his time writing poetry.

Far below the rank of senators, army leaders, wealthy businessmen, and famous writers were the ordinary people of the Roman Empire.

- **Plebeians** — This group included tenant farmers, artisans, construction workers, and storekeepers. Plebeian women ran shops and worked in a variety of trades. There were great differences within this rank of society. Some plebeians had successful small businesses and made a comfortable living. Others lived on the edge of poverty.

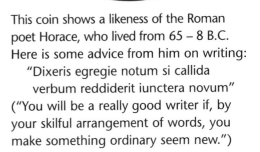

This coin shows a likeness of the Roman poet Horace, who lived from 65 – 8 B.C. Here is some advice from him on writing: "Dixeris egregie notum si callida verbum reddiderit iunctera novum" ("You will be a really good writer if, by your skilful arrangement of words, you make something ordinary seem new.")

- **The Unemployed** — As small farmers were crowded off the land and moved to cities hoping for work, a more or less permanent group of people living in poverty developed. Some managed to find odd jobs, but most depended on the state for their food.

- **Slaves** — Slaves had the lowest status. Within Italy alone, historians estimate that there were about three million slaves, who worked in farming, mining, construction, and household service. A small number of slaves were sent to the arena to fight as gladiators. Bloody and deadly contests between gladiators or with wild animals were a popular form of entertainment in both the Republic and the Roman Empire.

Although many slaves were treated harshly, those who were servants in the homes of wealthy families were more likely to be treated with kindness. Some were given an education and special training for a trade or profession. Also, educated slaves frequently acted as tutors for the children of wealthy families.

Some slaves accumulated enough money to buy their freedom. Sometimes owners gave slaves their freedom in return for faithful service.

REVOLT OF THE SLAVES

In this scene from the movie *Spartacus*, Spartacus and a Nubian gladiator prepare to fight.

In 73 B.C., a gladiator slave named Spartacus escaped and led an army of 70 000 slaves in a revolt that lasted for three years. He won several major battles against the Roman army, but was finally defeated and died in battle. As a punishment, 6000 of the rebellious slaves were crucified. The road that ran from Rome to Capua was lined with their crosses — a warning to future rebels.

The Roman general who defeated Spartacus was a man named Crassus. You can find the story of Spartacus in the life of Crassus written by the Greek historian Plutarch in the first century A.D.

ROMAN LEGIONNAIRES

When soldiers were needed in the early days of the Republic, citizens were called for service. Under Augustus, a professional army of about 400 000 soldiers was created. Serving in the Roman army was no longer a citizen's duty, but a chosen career.

Since Roman soldiers signed on for 20 years, it was important that they be well prepared. New recruits underwent a long period of training.

Legionnaires were the foot soldiers of the army, and were divided into four types of fighters:

- *velites* — carried spears and shields; came up between the rows of soldiers to launch stones at the enemy and then retreat

- *hastati* — were placed in the front line for a battle; wore light armour and carried two javelins and a sword

- *principes* — had swords, spears, and shields; went into battle behind the hastati

- *triarii* — the most experienced fighters; had full body armour and spears

Roman soldiers were well paid, but had to be prepared to buy their own weapons and food, and to march up to 30 km each day. Legionnaires were stationed throughout the Empire to protect and defend its borders. They lived in permanent forts that were always laid out in exactly the same way, and looked like small towns.

Daily Life: Homes, Food, and Clothing

Roman towns and cities were noisy and dirty. Rome itself was so crowded that vehicles were banned during the day. Most people lived in small one-room apartments built in large blocks up to six storeys high.

These apartment blocks often had shops on the ground floor. Most apartments had no running water or kitchens, so people used the town fountains and public toilets, and bought their meals at small food stands. Grain and bread were distributed to those without work or money.

Wealthy families could afford a separate house, and sometimes even a second home in the country, called a *villa*. Their city homes were low buildings with windowless walls to keep the noise out. The most elaborate homes had fountains and statues, artwork painted on the walls, and mosaic tile designs on the floors.

This is a room from a wealthy home in the city of Pompeii in southern Italy. On August 24, 79 A.D., when Mount Vesuvius erupted, Pompeii and the surrounding area were covered with almost 10 m of ash. The city lay buried for many centuries exactly as it was on the day of the disaster — the food that people were about to eat still on the table, the bodies of those who were suffocated by the smoke and ash lying in the streets. Many people come to see the ruins of this once-thriving Roman city.

Breakfast and lunch were simple meals — bread, fruit, cheese, and perhaps some fish and vegetables. The main meal was in the evening, and wealthy families had several courses prepared by servants — an appetizer (salad, fish, or eggs), a main course of meat and vegetables with spices, and to end the meal, a dessert of cake or fruits. Working-class families rarely ate meat, and lived mainly on bread, cheese, eggs, peas, olives, grapes, and vegetables.

For formal dress, all male citizens wore a toga, a large piece of plain woolen cloth wrapped around the body, with one end draped over the shoulder. Ordinary dress for both men and women was a woolen tunic. Married women wore a long dress, called a *stola*, over their tunic. In the colder parts of the Empire, people also needed woolen stockings and cloaks.

The family was the foundation of Roman society, and the father was its head. His authority over his wife, children, and slaves was absolute. When a child was born, it was the custom to lay the baby at the father's feet. If he picked the baby up, he was accepting the child as part of the family. If he did not, which rarely happened, the baby would be placed outside to die.

The wives of wealthy men occupied their time with running the household, spinning and weaving, and supervising their children. Plebeian women helped support their families as shopkeepers, millers, butchers, midwives, weavers, waitresses, and entertainers.

The children of wealthy families were sent to school at age seven and were taught reading, writing, and arithmetic. After reaching the age of 12 or 13, girls were tutored at home until they married, and boys were sent to a higher level school to study history, geography, astronomy, and literature. When boys became 16, they were considered adults, and began to train for a career.

Members of the Senate were identified by a broad purple stripe of their togas.

Religious Beliefs

The early Romans believed that everything around them had a spirit — trees, birds, lightning, grass, the harvest, the home, and so on. These spirits were neither good nor bad, but they could be helpful or harmful to people, depending on how they were treated. Certain rituals were intended to please the spirits.

This small shrine shows two households gods, called *lares,* on either side of the main household god.

When the Romans came in contact with the Etruscans, people living north of Rome, they added new beliefs and practices to their religion. They learned about gods with human forms, temples for making sacrifices, religious processions, and statues.

From the Etruscans the Romans also learned about foretelling the future and determining the will of the gods. They believed that the most reliable way of doing this was to examine the inner organs of an animal after it was sacrificed.

The Romans also came in contact with the many gods of Greece. They included most of these gods in their religion, but gave them Roman names. They also adopted many of the stories associated with the Greek gods.

At the head of the great family of Roman gods was Jupiter. He was the god of the sky and the protector of the Roman state. His wife, Juno, guarded women, and watched over marriage and childbirth. Some other important Roman gods were Venus, Mars, Minerva, Neptune, Diana, Mercury, and Ceres.

The Pantheon, built as a temple to honour all the Roman gods, is one of the most famous buildings in Rome. Its only source of light is an opening in its domed roof.

As the Empire expanded, the Romans came in contact with many new gods and goddesses. The goddess Isis from Egypt, the Persian god Mithras, and the goddess Cybele had followers among the Romans. The Romans were generally open-minded about foreign gods and religious practices, but only if these did not threaten the official religion of the Empire.

Two groups of religious believers caused the Romans serious concern. The first was the Jewish people, who lived under Roman rule after Palestine was conquered in 63 B.C. Their belief in one God and their religious customs seemed strange to the Romans, but were tolerated. Emperor Augustus even decreed that Jewish places of worship were to be protected. Because of Jewish uprisings in the province of Judea, however, the Temple of Jerusalem was destroyed in 70 A.D., and the Jews were forcibly expelled from Palestine.

The second group was the Christians. Because of their belief that God alone was to be worshipped, many refused to burn incense in front of a statue of the emperor, a common ritual in the Roman Empire. The Romans viewed this defiance as a serious act of disloyalty, and Christianity was banned. Christians were persecuted, and many were tortured and executed. Some were ripped apart by wild animals in the Colosseum — a horrible spectacle watched by an audience who came to be entertained.

In Rome itself, Christians built underground burial tunnels called *catacombs* in which the bodies of many martyrs were laid to rest. Several hundred years later, they began to use the catacombs as places to celebrate the Eucharist. There are more than 35 of these excavated tunnels. Inscriptions and paintings on catacomb walls help us learn about early Christian art and symbols. Some of the most common are a cross, the Good Shepherd, an anchor, and a fish.

The symbol of a fish was probably a secret code. The first letters from the Greek words, **I**esous **C**hristos **TH**eou **U**ios **S**oter (Jesus Christ, Son of God, Saviour) spell the word **ICTHUS**, which is the Greek word for fish.

Christians endured more than 200 years of terrible persecution. But their suffering ended in 313 A.D. when the Roman emperor Constantine became a Christian, and made Christianity the official religion of the Empire. Rome itself became a city of great importance for Christians, since it was here that St. Peter and St. Paul were put to death. The Pope, who is the head of the Catholic Church, is the Bishop of Rome.

In the centuries after the fall of the Roman Empire, the Christian faith spread through Europe. Today there are almost two billion Christians all around the world.

Achievements of the Roman Empire

The Roman Empire of the west collapsed, but its heritage was not lost. The traditions and achievements of Rome were passed on by the Eastern Roman Empire and by the Roman Catholic Church:

- The Eastern Roman Empire, which came to be known as the Byzantine Empire, continued to exist for almost 1000 years after the fall of Rome. The Byzantine Empire followed many of the traditions of Rome — its form of government with an emperor, senate, and large civil service; Roman law; an army similar to that of the Western Empire.

Justinian was the emperor of the Eastern Empire from 527–565 A.D. One of his greatest contributions was his law code, which brought together all of the laws the Romans had developed since before the time of the Republic. This photograph of a mosaic shows Justinian and some of his advisers and priests.

- In the western part of the old Roman Empire, the Catholic Church kept the heritage of Rome alive. Church schools taught Latin, which became the language of education all over Europe. They also introduced students to the great works of ancient literature. Copies of these writings were made by monks and preserved in the libraries of monasteries.

Civilizations rise and fall, and sometimes they seem to disappear without a trace. But the influence of the Roman Empire was far too powerful for this to happen. Its outstanding achievements in law, language and literature, and in architecture and engineering continue to influence the Western world.

- **Roman law** — The great Roman writer Cicero wrote that a state without law is like a body without a mind. For the Romans, justice could not be achieved unless human rights were recognized, and the law was administered impartially. A person's influence or wealth should have no bearing on the outcome of a legal matter. Here are some examples from Justinian's Code of Roman Law that show this concern for justice and the rights of persons:

  No one suffers a penalty for what he thinks.
  No one may be forcibly removed from his own home.
  A father is not a competent witness for a son,
  nor a son for a father.
  In inflicting penalties, the age and experience of the
  guilty party must be taken into account.

  The influence of Roman law can be seen in the legal systems of many European countries. In Canada, the civil law code used in the province of Québec has its origin in Roman law.

- **Roman language and literature** — The people of the Empire spoke many languages, but the official language was Latin. After the fall of Rome, Latin continued to be used in literature, education, religion, and government for more than a thousand years. Christian missionaries introduced Latin to areas of Europe that had never been under Roman rule. In the great universities of the Middle Ages, people from many different countries could learn together and exchange ideas because they shared a common language.

  Over many centuries, Latin gave birth to a number of different languages that are spoken today: Italian, French, Spanish, Portuguese, and Romanian. English also shows the influence of Latin. Here are a few examples of Latin words that are so similar to English that you will be able to figure them out: *disciplina, fortitudo, delibero, inconsideratus.*

  Roman literature, and especially its poetry, is still read and studied today. Great epic poems like Vergil's *Aeneid* influenced generations of writers.

- **Architecture and engineering** — The Romans built their roads, public buildings, baths, aqueducts, and bridges all over the Empire. They added strength to their buildings through the use of cement. They were the first people to use this wet mixture of stone, lime, and sand for construction. For the design of their buildings, the Romans often borrowed ideas, especially from the Greeks. But the engineering genius of these structures was all their own.

Romans built their roads with great care. A deep foundation was dug and then filled in with several layers of stones, pebbles, and earth. This present-day photo shows the Appian Way, perhaps Rome's most famous road. It was along this road that Spartacus and his followers were crucified.

One of the greatest gifts of the Romans was their practicality. They appreciated and built impressive structures like the Colosseum, but they also understood everyday needs for fresh water, decent roads, public baths, and sewers to eliminate waste. For many people, one important consequence of being conquered by Rome was that they lived far more comfortably than they had in the past.

The Romans never doubted their destiny, and perhaps they were justified in their self-confidence. There was much that was brutal and harsh in the Roman world, but that same world nurtured ideals that still inspire us today — the rights of persons, equality under the law, government as a matter for the people. The Empire they established did not survive, but the civilization they created continues to influence our way of life.

The End of the Journey

You have come to the end of your journey to the country of the past. During your travels you have visited civilizations in Africa, the Americas, Asia, and Europe. The natural environments in which these civilizations developed are quite different — from the Nile valley of Africa to the rain forests of Central America, from the lands circling the Mediterranean Sea to the river valleys of China. You have seen how human beings are able to adapt to a variety of environments in order to meet their basic needs and create a home for themselves in the world. This ability is the starting point of each of the civilizations you have studied.

But God's gifts of intelligence and creativity drive people to go far beyond meeting their basic needs. From ancient times to the present, human beings have:

- used their gifts to create something that will survive after they are gone — magnificent buildings, technologies that are passed on to the next generation, beautiful sculptures and paintings, detailed codes of law, monuments inscribed with great deeds, written records of their knowledge, experiences, and feelings.

The Greek playwright Sophocles lived almost 2500 years ago. People today are still moved by the power of his words. This photograph shows a scene from his play, *Oedipus the King,* performed in the Colosseum in Rome in 1999.

- asked questions about life and death, happiness and misery, good and evil, and the purpose of their existence.

- experienced the mystery of something greater than themselves and their existence on the earth.

During your journey, you have seen many examples of the marvels that we human beings are capable of creating. You have also seen examples of injustice and disrespect for human life — slavery, human sacrifice, terrible cruelty, abuses of power. Evil is present in all societies. Human history is not only a record of remarkable and lasting achievements, but also a painful reminder of our inclination to sin — to dominate rather than to serve, to treat persons as if they were things, to resort to violence rather than seek peace, and to be so concerned with our own needs and comfort that we ignore the misery of others.

When people are members of a society in which slavery, human sacrifice, or violent entertainment are a normal part of life, it is difficult for them to see how wrong such practices are. Because we are social beings, we are strongly influenced by the attitudes and traditions of the society in which we live. This was true for the civilizations you have explored, and it is true for us.

It takes people of wisdom and courage to rise above their society's customs and traditions, and see that reforms are needed — people like Bartolome de Las Casas, the Spanish priest who recognized that slavery was wrong and spent his life fighting for the rights of the people of the Americas. His inspiration was the vision of life proclaimed in the Gospel.

As followers of Jesus, we, too, have been given the responsibility to use our gifts to work for a civilization that reflects the goodness of our Creator. This work begins in our homes, classrooms, workplaces, and communities. Each one of us is called to prepare the way for the Kingdom of God where perfect love, justice, and peace will last forever.

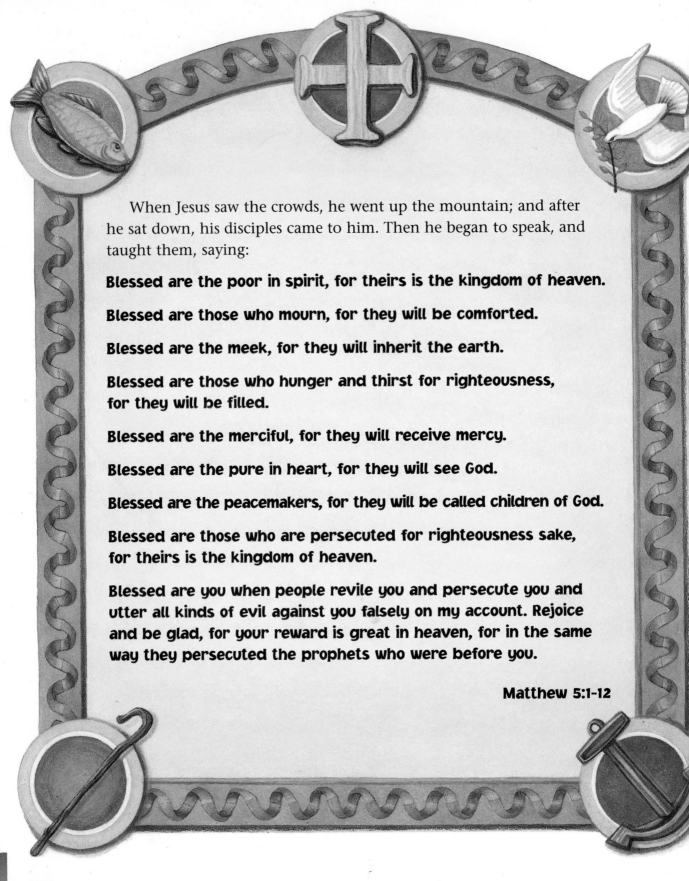

When Jesus saw the crowds, he went up the mountain; and after he sat down, his disciples came to him. Then he began to speak, and taught them, saying:

Blessed are the poor in spirit, for theirs is the kingdom of heaven.

Blessed are those who mourn, for they will be comforted.

Blessed are the meek, for they will inherit the earth.

Blessed are those who hunger and thirst for righteousness, for they will be filled.

Blessed are the merciful, for they will receive mercy.

Blessed are the pure in heart, for they will see God.

Blessed are the peacemakers, for they will be called children of God.

Blessed are those who are persecuted for righteousness sake, for theirs is the kingdom of heaven.

Blessed are you when people revile you and persecute you and utter all kinds of evil against you falsely on my account. Rejoice and be glad, for your reward is great in heaven, for in the same way they persecuted the prophets who were before you.

Matthew 5:1-12